First published in this edition 1995

© **HarperCollins Publishers 1995**

ISBN 0 00 470731-1

text
Mary Wade

editor
Joyce Littlejohn

series editor
Lorna Sinclair Knight

editorial management
Vivian Marr

*A catalogue record for this book
is available from the British Library*

*Typeset by Latimer Trend Ltd.,
Plymouth*

*Printed in Great Britain by
HarperCollins Manufacturing, Glasgow*

COLLINS
POCKET
LATIN
GRAMMAR
& VERB TABLES

HarperCollins*Publishers*

This book is designed to help pupils and students of Latin to understand the grammar of the language. For beginners, the book provides an introduction to and explanation of the basic forms. More advanced students will find it an invaluable guide for reference and revision.

All parts of speech (nouns, pronouns, adjectives etc) are treated separately and clearly explained for the benefit of learners. Differences in usage are illustrated by extensive examples from many Latin authors.

A special section on word order in Latin, one of the greatest problems for students and pupils, has been included to guide the learner through both simple and compound sentences.

For ease of reference, all necessary structures, such as Indirect Statement, Conditional Sentences etc, have been listed under Contents. Each is then explained, for both English and Latin usage, to show the learner how to recognize the structure and translate it into English. Further examples of all structures are provided, for practice.

Handy, practical hints are given in the section on Translation Guidelines, to highlight the more common problems that confront students, and to assist in translation.

The final part of the grammar section lists the many "false friends" or confusable words that often lead students and pupils astray when translating from Latin. This section is of particular importance for examination candidates.

Tables of regular verbs provide information on verb formation and usage, while unique verbs are given in full with their meanings. A special feature of the grammar is a list of the 400 most common verbs, both regular and irregular. Irregular parts of verbs are highlighted and the conjugation number of each listed, so that by referring to the table indicated by this number any part of the verb may be deduced.

4 CONTENTS

CONTENTS 5

6 CONTENTS

Abbreviations used

abl	ablative	**m, masc**	masculine
acc	accusative	**nt, neut**	neuter
adv	adverb	**nom**	nominative
conj	conjunction	**pl**	plural
dat	dative	**plup**	pluperfect
dep	deponent	**p(p)**	page(s)
f, fem	feminine	**prep**	preposition
gen	genitive	**pron**	pronoun
indic	indicative	**sing**	singular
intrans	intransitive	**voc**	vocative

Nouns

A noun is the name of a person, thing or quality.

Gender

- In Latin, as in English, the gender of nouns, representing persons or living creatures, is decided by meaning. Nouns denoting male people and animals are masculine

vir	a man
Gaius	Gaius
cervus	stag

- Nouns denoting female people and animals are feminine

femina	a woman
Cornelia	Cornelia
cerva	doe/hind

- However, the gender of things or qualities in Latin is decided by the ending of the noun.

anulus (ring) *masc*
sapientia (wisdom) *fem*
barba (beard) *fem*
gaudium (joy) *nt*

Number

- Nouns may be singular, denoting one, or plural, denoting two or more. This is shown by change of ending

	sing	*pl*
	ter**ra** (land)	ter**rae**
	mo**dus** (way)	mo**di**
	o**pus** (work)	o**pera**

Cases

- There are six cases in Latin, expressing the relationship of the noun to the other words in the sentence.

Nominative
the subject of the verb: **Caesar** died

Vocative
addressing someone/thing: Welcome, **Alexander**

Accusative
the object of the verb: The cat ate **the mouse**

Genitive
belonging to someone/thing: The home **of my friend**

Dative
the indirect object of the verb: I gave the book **to my son**

Ablative
says by, with or from whom/what: This was agreed **by the Senate**

Declensions

- Latin nouns are divided into five groups or declensions by the ending of their stems. Each declension has six cases, both singular and plural, denoted by different endings. The endings of the genitive singular case help to distinguish the different declensions.

	STEMS	GENITIVE SINGULAR	
1st	Declension	-a	-ae
2nd	Declension	-ŏ or u	-ī
3rd	Declension	-i, u, **consonant**	-is
4th	Declension	-ŭ	-ūs
5th	Declension	-ē	-ēi

First Declension

- All nouns end in -**a** in the nominative case and all are feminine except when the noun indicates a male, *eg* **poēta** (a poet), **agricola** (a farmer), *etc.*

	SINGULAR		PLURAL	
Nom	fēmin**a**	the woman	fēmin**ae**	women
Voc	fēmin**a**	o woman	fēmin**ae**	o women
Acc	fēmin**am**	the woman	fēmin**ās**	women
Gen	fēmin**ae**	of the woman	fēmin**ārum**	of the women
Dat	fēmin**ae**	to/for the woman	fēmin**īs**	to/for the women
Abl	fēmin**ā**	by/with/ from the woman	fēmin**īs**	by/with/ from the women

- Note that **dea** (goddess) and **filia** (daughter), have their dative and ablative plurals **deābus** and **filiābus**

Declensions (contd)

Second Declension

- Nouns of the second declension end in **-us**, or a few in **-er** or **-r**. All are masculine. Those few which end in **-um** are neuter.

	SINGULAR		PLURAL	
Nom	serv**us**	*slave*	serv**ī**	*slaves*
Voc	serv**e**		serv**ī**	
Acc	serv**um**		serv**ōs**	
Gen	serv**ī**		serv**ōrum**	
Dat	serv**ō**		serv**īs**	
Abl	serv**o**		serv**īs**	

	SINGULAR		PLURAL	
Nom	pu**er**	*boy*	puer**ī**	*boys*
Voc	pu**er**		puer**ī**	
Acc	puer**um**		puer**ōs**	
Gen	puer**ī**		puer**ōrum**	
Dat	puer**ō**		puer**īs**	
Abl	puer**ō**		puer**īs**	

	SINGULAR		PLURAL	
Nom	bell**um**	*war*	bell**a**	*wars*
Voc	bell**um**		bell**a**	
Acc	bell**um**		bell**a**	
Gen	bell**ī**		bell**ōrum**	
Dat	bell**ō**		bell**īs**	
Abl	bell**ō**		bell**īs**	

- Note that proper names ending in **-ius** have vocative in **-ī**, **o Vergīlī** – o Virgil!

- **deus** (god), has an alternative vocative **deus**, and plural forms **di** in nominative and **dis** in dative and ablative.

Third Declension

This is the largest group of nouns and may be divided into two broad categories, stems ending in a consonant and those ending in -**i**. All genders in this declension must be learnt.

Consonant Stems

- ending in -**l**

  consul, -is *m* (consul)

	SINGULAR	PLURAL
Nom	cōnsul	cōnsul**ēs**
Voc	cōnsul	cōnsul**ēs**
Acc	cōnsul**em**	cōnsul**ēs**
Gen	cōnsul**is**	cōnsul**um**
Dat	cōnsul**ī**	cōnsul**ibus**
Abl	cōnsul**e**	cōnsul**ibus**

- ending in -**n**

  legio, -onis *f* (legion)

	SINGULAR	PLURAL
Nom	legiō	legiōn**ēs**
Voc	legiō	legiōn**ēs**
Acc	legiōn**em**	legiōn**ēs**
Gen	legiōn**is**	legiōn**um**
Dat	legiōn**ī**	legiōn**ibus**
Abl	legiōn**e**	legiōn**ibus**

Continued

Declensions (contd)

flumen, -inis *nt* (river)

	SINGULAR	PLURAL
Nom	flūmen	flūmin**a**
Voc	flūmen	flūmin**a**
Acc	flūmen	flūmin**a**
Gen	flūmin**is**	flūmin**um**
Dat	flūmin**ī**	flūmin**ibus**
Abl	flūmin**e**	flūmin**ibus**

- Note that the genitive plural of these nouns ends in -**um**.

- Stems ending in -**i**

civis, -is *m/f* (citizen)

	SINGULAR	PLURAL
Nom	cīv**is**	cīv**ēs**
Voc	cīv**is**	cīv**ēs**
Acc	cīv**em**	cīv**ēs**
Gen	cīv**is**	cīv**ium**
Dat	cīv**ī**	cīv**ibus**
Abl	cīv**e**	cīv**ibus**

- Note that these nouns have genitive plural in -**ium**.

Neuter Nouns

mare, -is *nt* (sea)

	SINGULAR	PLURAL
Nom	mar**e**	mar**ia**
Voc	mar**e**	mar**ia**
Acc	mar**e**	mar**ia**
Gen	mar**is**	mar**ium**
Dat	mari	mar**ibus**
Abl	marī	mar**ibus**

animal, -is *nt* (animal)

	SINGULAR	PLURAL
Nom	animal	animāl**ia**
Voc	animal	animāl**ia**
Acc	animal	animāl**ia**
Gen	animāl**is**	animāl**ium**
Dat	animālī	animāl**ibus**
Abl	animālī	animāl**ibus**

- Note that the ablative singular of these neuter nouns ends in -ī.

- Nominative, vocative and accusative singular endings of neuter nouns are identical.

- Nominative, vocative and accusative plural endings of neuter nouns in **all** declensions end in -ă.

Continued

Declensions (contd)

Monosyllabic Consonant Stems

The following have their genitive plural in **-ium**:

arx, arcis *f* (citadel)	– arc**ium** (of citadels)
gēns, gentis *f* (race)	– gent**ium** (of races)
mōns, montis *m* (mountain)	– mont**ium** (of mountains)
nox, noctis *f* (night)	– noct**ium** (of nights)
pōns, pontis *m* (bridge)	– pont**ium** (of bridges)
urbs, urbis *f* (city)	– urb**ium** (of cities)

Fourth Declension

Nouns in this declension end in **-us** in the nominative singular and are mainly masculine. A few end in **-u** and are neuter.

exercitus, -ūs *m* (army)

	SINGULAR	PLURAL
Nom	exercit**us**	exercit**ūs**
Voc	exercit**us**	exercit**ūs**
Acc	exercit**um**	exercit**ūs**
Gen	exercit**ūs**	exercit**uum**
Dat	exercit**uī**	exercit**ibus**
Abl	exercit**ū**	exercit**ibus**

genū, -ūs *nt* (knee)

	SINGULAR	PLURAL
Nom	gen**ū**	gen**ua**
Voc	gen**ū**	gen**ua**
Acc	gen**ū**	gen**ua**
Gen	gen**ūs**	gen**uum**
Dat	gen**ū**	gen**ibus**
Abl	gen**ū**	gen**ibus**

- Note that a few common nouns are feminine, *eg* **domus** (house), **manus** (hand), **Idus** (Ides *or* 15th of the month).

- The form **domī** (at home) is an old form called locative. **domō** (from home) *abl sing*, **domōs** *acc pl* and **domōrum** *gen pl* are also used besides the fourth declension forms of **domus** (house).

Fifth Declension

There are only a few nouns in this declension. All end in -**ēs** in the nominative case. Most are feminine, but **diēs** (day) and **meridiēs** (midday) are masculine.

diēs, -diēī *m* (day)

	SINGULAR	PLURAL
Nom	diēs	diēs
Voc	diēs	diēs
Acc	diem	diēs
Gen	diēī	diērum
Dat	diēī	diēbus
Abl	diē	diēbus

Cases

Use Of Cases

Nominative Case

The nominative case is used where:

- the noun is the **subject** of the verb (→**1**)
- the noun is a **complement** (→**2**)
- the noun is **in apposition** to the subject (→**3**)

Accusative Case

The accusative case is used:

- for the **direct object** of the verb (→**4**)
- with verbs of teaching and asking which take accusative of person and thing (→**5**)
- Verbs of naming, making *etc* take two accusatives for the same person or thing (→**6**)
- in exclamations (→**7**)
- to show extent of space (→**8**)
- to show extent of time (→**9**)
- to show motion to a place or country usually with a preposition (→**10**)
- to show motion towards, without a preposition, before names of towns and small islands (→**11**)

    Note also: **domum** (home), **rus** (to the country), **foras** (outside)

- for an object with similar meaning to the verb (*cognate*) (→**12**)

Continued

1 **Sextus** ridet
Sextus laughs

2 Romulus **rex** factus est
Romulus was made king

3 Marcus Annius, **eques Romanus**, hoc dicit
Marcus Annius, a Roman businessman, says this

4 canis **baculum** petit
the dog fetches the stick

5 **puerum litteras** docebo
I shall teach the boy literature

6 **Ancum Martium regem** populus creavit
The people made Ancus Martius king

7 o **tempora**, o **mores**
what times, what conduct!

8 murus decem **pedes** altus est
the wall is 10 foot high

9 Troia decem **annos** obsessa est
Troy was under siege for 10 years

10 **ad Hispaniam** effugerunt
they escaped to Spain

11 **Athenas** legati missi sunt
Ambassadors were sent to Athens

12 **vitam** bonam **vixit**
he lived a good life

Cases (contd)

Dative Case

- Indirect object (*ie* to or for whom an action is performed) (→**1**)

- used with verbs of obeying (**parēre**), resisting (**resistere**), pleasing (**placēre**), ordering (**imperāre**) *etc* (→**2**)

- verb compounds (beginning **ad-**, **ob-**, **prae-**, **sub-**) denoting helping or hindering take dative (→**3**)

  adesse – come to help
  subvenire – help

- indicates possession (→**4**)

- is used with adjectives meaning "like" (**similis**), "fit" (**aptus**), "near" (**proximus**) (→**5**)

- indicates a purpose (known as *predicative dative*) (→**6**)

- shows the agent of gerund/gerundive (→**7**)

Continued

1 pecuniam **domino** dedit
he gave the money to his master

2 maria terraeque **Deo** parent
land and sea obey God

3 Pompeius **hostibus** obstitit
Pompey opposed the enemy

4 Poppaea amica est **Marciae**
Poppaea is Marcia's friend

5 feles **tigri similis** est
the cat is like a tiger

6 nemo mihi **auxilio** est
there is no-one to help me

7 omnia erant agenda **nobis**
everything had to be done by us

Cases (contd)

Genitive Case

- Indicates possession (→**1**)
- Denotes part of a whole (→**2**)
- Indicates a quality, always with an adjective (→**3**)
- Is used as a predicate, where a person represents a quality (→**4**)
- Is used with superlatives (→**5**)
- Precedes **causa** and **gratia** (for the sake of) (→**6**)
- Is used after certain adjectives (→**7**)

> **sciens**   (knowing)
> **inscius**   (ignorant of)
> **cupidus**   (desiring)
> **particeps** (sharing) *etc*

- Is used with verbs of remembering (**memini**) and forgetting (**obliviscor**) (→**8**)
- Follows verbs of accusing, convicting *etc* (→**9**)
- Represents value or worth (→**10**)

Continued

1. domus **regis**
   the king's house

   uxor **Augusti**
   the wife of Augustus

2. quid **novi**
   what news?

   plus **cibi**
   more food

3. magnae **auctoritatis** es
   your reputation is great

4. **stulti est** hoc facere
   it is the mark of a fool to do this

5. Indus est **omnium fluminum** maximum
   the Indus is the greatest of all rivers

6. tu me **amoris causa** servavisti
   you saved me for love's sake

7. Verres, **cupidus pecuniae**, ex hereditate praedatus
   est
   Verres, greedy for money, robbed the estate

8. **mortis** memento
   remember death

9. ante **actarum rerum** Antonius accusatus est
   Antony was accused of previous offences

10. frumentum **minimi** vendidit
    he sold corn at the lowest price

    flocci non facio
    I don't care at all

Cases (contd)

Ablative Case

- Indicates place, usually with the preposition "in" (→**1**)
  Note, however: **totā Asiā** – throughout Asia
  terrā marīque – by land and sea

- Indicates motion from, or down from a place, usually with prepositions **ex**, **de**, **a(b)** (→**2**)

- Note prepositions are omitted before names of towns, small islands and **domo** (from home), **rure** (from the country), **foris** (from outside) (→**3**)

- Represents time when or within which something happens (→**4**)

- Indicates origin, sometimes with prepositions **in**, **ex**, **a(b)** (→**5**)

- Is used to show material from which something is made (→**6**)

- Indicates manner (how something is done), usually with **cum** when there is no adjective, and without **cum** when there is an adjective (→**7**)

- Is used with verbs of depriving, filling, needing and with **opus est** (→**8**)

- Is used with deponent verbs **utor** (use), **abutor** (abuse), **fungor** (accomplish), **potior** (gain possession of) (→**9**)

- States cause (→**10**)

- To form **ablative absolute**, where a noun in the ablative is combined with a participle or another noun or adjective in the same case, to form an idea independent of the rest of the sentence. This is equivalent to an adverbial clause (→**11**)

1 Milo **in urbe** mansit
Milo remained in the city

2 **de equo** cecidit
He fell down from his horse

praedam **ex urbe ornatissima** sustulit
He stole booty from the rich city

3 **domo** cucurrerunt servi
The slaves ran from the house

4 **hac nocte** Agricola obiit
Agricola died on this night

decem annis Lacedaimonii non haec confecerunt
The Spartans did not complete this task within 10 years

5 Romulus et Remus, **Marte nati**
Romulus and Remus, sons of Mars

flumina **in Caucaso monte** orta
Rivers rising in the Caucasus mountains

6 statua **ex auro** facta est
The statue was made of gold

7 mulieres **cum virtute** vixerunt
The women lived virtuously

summa celeritate Poeni regressi sunt
The Carthaginians retreated at top speed

8 aliquem **vita** privare   opus est mihi **divitiis**
to deprive someone of life   I need wealth

9 **vi** et **armis** usus est   **10** leo **fame** decessit
He used force of arms   The lion died of hunger

11 **exigua parte aestatis reliqua**, Caesar in Britanniam proficisci contendit
Although only a little of the summer remained, Caesar hurried to set out for Britain

Adjectives

An adjective adds a quality to the noun. It usually follows
the noun but sometimes comes before it for emphasis. The
adjective agrees with its noun in number, case and gender.

Gender
vir bonus (*masc*)	a good man
fēmina pulchra (*fem*)	a beautiful woman
bellum longum (*neut*)	a long war

Number
virī bonī (*pl*)	good men
fēminae pulchrae (*pl*)	beautiful women
bella longa (*pl*)	long wars

Case
virō bonō (*dat sing*)	for a good man
fēminās pulchrās (*acc pl*)	beautiful women
bellī longī (*gen sing*)	of a long war

- Adjectives are declined like nouns and usually arranged
  in two groups:
  1. those with endings of the first and second de-
     clensions
  2. those with endings of the third declension

First and Second Declensions

bonus, bona, bonum (good)

SINGULAR

	Masc	Fem	Neut
Nom	bonus	bona	bonum
Voc	bone	bona	bonum
Acc	bonum	bonam	bonum
Gen	bonī	bonae	bonī
Dat	bonō	bonae	bonō
Abl	bonō	bonā	bonō

PLURAL

	Masc	Fem	Neut
Nom	bonī	bonae	bona
Voc	bonī	bonae	bona
Acc	bonōs	bonās	bona
Gen	bonōrum	bonārum	bonōrum
Dat	bonīs	bonīs	bonīs
Abl	bonīs	bonīs	bonīs

Declensions (contd)

miser, misera, miserum (unhappy)

	Masc	Fem	Neut
		SINGULAR	
	Masc	Fem	Neut
Nom	mis**er**	miser**a**	miser**um**
Voc	mis**er**	miser**a**	miser**um**
Acc	miser**um**	miser**am**	miser**um**
Gen	miser**ī**	miser**ae**	miser**ī**
Dat	miser**ō**	miser**ae**	miser**ō**
Abl	miser**ō**	miser**ā**	miser**ō**

	Masc	Fem	Neut
		PLURAL	
	Masc	Fem	Neut
Nom	miser**ī**	miser**ae**	miser**a**
Voc	miser**ī**	miser**ae**	miser**a**
Acc	miser**ōs**	miser**ās**	miser**a**
Gen	miser**ōrum**	miser**ārum**	miser**ōrum**
Dat	miser**īs**	miser**īs**	miser**īs**
Abl	miser**īs**	miser**īs**	miser**īs**

● **liber** (free) and **tener** (tender) are declined like **miser**

pulcher, pulchra, pulchrum (beautiful)

SINGULAR

	Masc	Fem	Neut
Nom	pulch**er**	pulch**ra**	pulch**rum**
Voc	pulch**er**	pulch**ra**	pulch**rum**
Acc	pulch**rum**	pulch**ram**	pulch**rum**
Gen	pulch**rī**	pulch**rae**	pulch**rī**
Dat	pulch**rō**	pulch**rae**	pulch**rō**
Abl	pulch**rō**	pulch**rā**	pulch**rō**

PLURAL

	Masc	Fem	Neut
Nom	pulch**rī**	pulch**rae**	pulch**ra**
Voc	pulch**rī**	pulch**rae**	pulch**ra**
Acc	pulch**rōs**	pulch**rās**	pulch**ra**
Gen	pulch**rōrum**	pulch**rārum**	pulch**rōrum**
Dat	pulch**rīs**	pulch**rīs**	pulch**rīs**
Abl	pulch**rīs**	pulch**rīs**	pulch**rīs**

- **aeger** (sick), **crēber** (frequent), **integer** (whole), **niger** (black), **piger** (slow) and **sacer** (sacred) are declined like **pulcher**

Declensions (contd)

- The following group of adjectives form their genitive
  singular in **-ius** and dative singular in **-i**:

alius, -a, -ud	another
alter, altera, alterum	one of two
neuter, neutra, neutrum	neither
nūllus, -a, -um	none
sōlus, -a, -um	alone
tōtus, -a, -um	whole
ūllus, -a, -um	any
ūnus, -a, -um	one
uter, utra, utrum	which of two?

solus (alone)

SINGULAR

	Masc	Fem	Neut
Nom	sol**us**	sol**a**	sol**um**
Acc	sol**um**	sol**am**	sol**um**
Gen	sol**ius**	sol**ius**	sol**ius**
Dat	sol**i**	sol**i**	sol**i**
Abl	sol**o**	sol**a**	sol**o**

PLURAL

	Masc	Fem	Neut
Nom	sol**i**	sol**ae**	sol**a**
Acc	sol**os**	sol**as**	sol**a**
Gen	sol**orum**	sol**arum**	sol**orum**
Dat	sol**is**	sol**is**	sol**is**
Abl	sol**is**	sol**is**	sol**is**

Third Declension

Adjectives of the third declension, like nouns, may be divided into two broad types, those with consonant stems and those with vowel stems in **-i**.

Consonant Stems

These have **one** ending in nominative singular.

prūdēns (wise)

		SINGULAR	
	Masc	Fem	Neut
Nom	prūd**ēns**	prūd**ēns**	prūd**ēns**
Voc	prūd**ēns**	prūd**ēns**	prūd**ēns**
Acc	prūdent**em**	prūdent**em**	prūd**ēns**
Gen	prūdent**is**	prūdent**is**	prūdent**is**
Dat	prūdent**ī**	prūdent**ī**	prūdent**ī**
Abl	prūdent**ī**	prūdent**ī**	prūdent**ī**

		PLURAL	
	Masc	Fem	Neut
Nom	prūdent**ēs**	prūdent**ēs**	prūdent**ia**
Voc	prūdent**ēs**	prūdent**ēs**	prūdent**ia**
Acc	prūdent**ēs**	prūdent**ēs**	prūdent**ia**
Gen	prūdent**ium**	prūdent**ium**	prūdent**ium**
Dat	prūdent**ibus**	prūdent**ibus**	prūdent**ibus**
Abl	prūdent**ibus**	prūdent**ibus**	prūdent**ibus**

- **dīligēns** (careful), **innocēns** (innocent), **potēns** (powerful), **frequēns** (frequent), **ingēns** (huge) are declined like **prūdēns**

Declensions (contd)

amāns (loving)

SINGULAR

	Masc	Fem	Neut
Nom	amāns	amāns	amāns
Voc	amāns	amāns	amāns
Acc	amantem	amantem	amāns
Gen	amantis	amantis	amantis
Dat	amantī	amantī	amantī
Abl	amante	amante	amante

PLURAL

	Masc	Fem	Neut
Nom	amantēs	amantēs	amantia
Voc	amantēs	amantēs	amantia
Acc	amantēs	amantēs	amantia
Gen	amantium	amantium	amantium
Dat	amantibus	amantibus	amantibus
Abl	amantibus	amantibus	amantibus

- All Present participles are declined like **amans**, although Present participles of the other conjugations end in **-ēns**
- When participles are used as adjectives **-ī** is used instead of **-e** in ablative singular case

fēlix (lucky)

	Masc	SINGULAR Fem	Neut
Nom	fēlix	fēlix	fēlix
Voc	fēlix	fēlix	fēlix
Acc	fēlicem	fēlicem	fēlix
Gen	fēlicis	fēlicis	fēlicis
Dat	fēlicī	fēlicī	fēlicī
Abl	fēlicī	fēlicī	fēlicī

	Masc	PLURAL Fem	Neut
Nom	fēlicēs	fēlicēs	fēlicia
Voc	fēlicēs	fēlicēs	fēlicia
Acc	fēlicēs	fēlicēs	fēlicia
Gen	fēlicium	fēlicium	fēlicium
Dat	fēlicibus	fēlicibus	fēlicibus
Abl	fēlicibus	fēlicibus	fēlicibus

audāx (bold) and ferōx (fierce) are declined like fēlix

- Note that all the above adjectives have the same case endings in all genders except for the neuter accusative singular and the neuter nominative, vocative and accusative plural.

Declensions (contd)

Vowel Stems

The following adjectives have **two** endings in nominative singular, one for masculine and feminine, one for neuter.

fortis, forte (brave)

SINGULAR

	Masc	Fem	Neut
Nom	fort**is**	fort**is**	fort**e**
Voc	fort**is**	fort**is**	fort**e**
Acc	fort**em**	fort**em**	fort**e**
Gen	fort**is**	fort**is**	fort**is**
Dat	fort**ī**	fort**ī**	fort**ī**
Abl	fort**ī**	fort**ī**	fort**ī**

PLURAL

	Masc	Fem	Neut
Nom	fort**ēs**	fort**ēs**	fort**ia**
Voc	fort**ēs**	fort**ēs**	fort**ia**
Acc	fort**ēs**	fort**ēs**	fort**ia**
Gen	fort**ium**	fort**ium**	fort**ium**
Dat	fort**ibus**	fort**ibus**	fort**ibus**
Abl	fort**ibus**	fort**ibus**	fort**ibus**

- **brevis** (short), **facilis** (easy), **gravis** (heavy), **levis** (light), **omnis** (all), **tristis** (sad), **turpis** (disgraceful), **talis** (of such a kind), and **qualis** (of which kind), are declined like **fortis**.

The following adjectives have **three** endings in nominative singular.

ācer, ācris, ācre (sharp)

	SINGULAR		
	Masc	Fem	Neut
Nom	ācer	ācris	ācre
Voc	ācer	ācris	ācre
Acc	ācrem	ācrem	ācre
Gen	ācris	ācris	ācris
Dat	ācrī	ācrī	ācrī
Abl	ācrī	ācrī	ācrī

	PLURAL		
	Masc	Fem	Neut
Nom	ācrēs	ācrēs	ācria
Voc	ācrēs	ācrēs	ācria
Acc	ācrēs	ācrēs	ācria
Gen	ācrium	ācrium	ācrium
Dat	ācribus	ācribus	ācribus
Abl	ācribus	ācribus	ācribus

- **alacer** (lively), **equester** (of cavalry), and **volucer** (winged), are declined like **acer**, and **celer** (swift), declines similarly, but keeps **-e-** throughout (*eg* **celer, celeris, celere**)

Use of Adjectives

There are two ways of using adjectives.

- They can be used **attributively**, where the adjective in English comes before the noun: the new car

- An attributive adjective in Latin usually follows its noun but may sometimes come before it with a change of meaning (→**1**)

- They can be used **predicatively**, where the adjective comes after the verb: the car is new (→**2**)

- If an adjective describes two nouns, it agrees in gender with the nearer (→**3**)

- When an adjective describes two subjects of different sex it is often masculine plural (→**4**)

- When an adjective describes two subjects representing things without life it is often neuter plural (→**5**)

1 res **parvae**
small things

in parvis rebus
in unimportant matters

civis **Romanus** sum
I am a Roman citizen

2 Servi erant **fideles**
The slaves were faithful

3 Antonius, vir consilii **magni** et prudentiae
Antony, a man of great wisdom and prudence

4 frater et soror sunt **timidi**
Brother and sister are frightened

5 Calor et ventus per artus **praesentia** erant
Warmth and wind were present in the limbs

Comparative and Superlative

Adjectives also have comparative forms *eg* I am **luckier**
than you, and superlative forms *eg* the **noblest** Roman of
them all.

Formation

● The comparative is formed by adding **-ior** (*masc* and
fem) and **-ius** (*neut*) to the consonant stem of the
adjective and the superlative by adding **-issimus, -a,
-um** to the stem:

POSITIVE	**altus**	high
	audāx	bold
	brevis	short
	prūdēns	wise
COMPARATIVE	**altior**	higher
	audācior	bolder
	brevior	shorter
	prūdentior	wiser
SUPERLATIVE	**altissimus**	highest
	audācissimus	boldest
	brevissimus	shortest
	prūdentissimus	wisest

Continued

- If the adjective ends in **-er** (*in masc nom sing*) add **-rimus** to form the superlative.

POSITIVE	**ācer**	sharp
	celer	swift
	miser	unhappy
	pulcher	beautiful
COMPARATIVE	**ācrior**	sharper
	celerior	swifter
	miserior	more unhappy
	pulchrior	more beautiful
SUPERLATIVE	**ācerrimus**	sharpest
	celerrimus	swiftest
	miserrimus	most unhappy
	pulcherrimus	most beautiful

- Six adjectives ending in **-ilis** (*in masc nom sing*) add **-limus** to the stem to form the superlative.

POSITIVE	**facilis**	easy
	difficilis	difficult
	similis	like
	dissimilis	unlike
	gracilis	slight
	humilis	low
COMPARATIVE	**facilior**	easier
	difficilior	more difficult
	similior	more like
	dissimilior	more unlike
	gracilior	more slight
	humilior	lower
SUPERLATIVE	**facillimus**	easiest
	difficillimus	most difficult
	simillimus	most like
	dissimillimus	most unlike
	gracillimus	most slight
	humillimus	lowest

Comparative and Superlative (contd)

Irregular comparison

● Some adjectives have irregular comparative and superlative forms:

POSITIVE

bonus	good
malus	bad
parvus	small
magnus	big
multus	much
multī	many

COMPARATIVE

melior	better
pēior	worse
minor	smaller
māior	bigger
plūs	more
plūrēs	more

SUPERLATIVE

optimus	best
pessimus	worst
minimus	smallest, least
māximus	biggest
plūrimus	most
plūrimī	most

Continued

- Note that all adjectives ending in **-us** preceded by a vowel (except those ending in **-quus**) form comparative and superlative thus:

idōneus	suitable
magis idōneus	more suitable
māximē idōneus	most suitable

but

antīquus	old
antīquior	older
antīquissimus	oldest

- Note the following comparatives and superlatives where there is no positive form:

exterior	outer	**extrēmus**	furthest
inferior	lower	**infīmus** *or* **īmus**	lowest
superior	upper, higher	**suprēmus** *or* **summus**	highest
posterior	later	**postrēmus**	latest

Comparative and Superlative (contd)

Declension of Comparative and Superlative

- All comparatives decline like adjectives of the third declension.

	SINGULAR		PLURAL	
	Masc/Fem	Neut	Masc/Fem	Neut
Nom	**altior**	**altius**	**altiōrēs**	**altiōra**
Voc	**altior**	**altius**	**altiōrēs**	**altiōra**
Acc	**altiōrem**	**altius**	**altiōrēs**	**altiōra**
Gen	**altiōris**	**altiōris**	**altiōrum**	**altiōrum**
Dat	**altiōrī**	**altiōrī**	**altiōribus**	**altiōribus**
Abl	**altiōre**	**altiōre**	**altiōribus**	**altiōribus**

- Note ablative singular in **-e**.
- All superlatives decline like adjectives of first and second declensions (*eg* **bonus, bona, bonum**).

Use

- The comparative is often followed by **quam** (than), or the thing or person compared is given in the ablative case (→**1**)

- Sometimes the comparative can be translated by "rather" or "quite" (→**2**)

- The comparative is often strengthened by "**multo**" (→**3**)

- Sometimes the superlative can be translated by "very", or even as a positive adjective in English (→**4**)

- "**quam**" with the superlative means "as ... as possible" (→**5**)

1 Marcus est **altior quam soror**
Marcus est **altior sorore**
Marcus is taller than his sister

2 Gallus erat **fortior**
the Gaul was rather brave

3 **multo carior**
much dearer

4 **vir sapientissimus**
a very wise man

integerrima vita
of virtuous life

5 **quam paucissimi**
as few people as possible

Adverbs

An adverb modifies a verb, adjective, another adverb or a noun. It answers questions such as "how?", "when?", "why?", "where?", "to what extent?".

Formation

- Some are formed from nouns *eg* **furtim** (stealthily) or pronouns **aliās** (at other times) but most are formed from adjectives.

- Accusative singular neuter of adjectives of extent:

multum	much	**nimium**	too much
paulum	a little	**aliquantum**	somewhat
prīmum	first	**cēterum**	for the rest

- Adjectives in -**us** and -**er** change to -**e**:

altē	highly	**miserē**	wretchedly

- Ablative forms of these adjectives in -**o** or -**a**:

certē *or* **certō**	certainly	**verē**	in truth
dextrā	on the right	**verō**	certainly

- Adjectives of the third declension add -**ter**/-**iter**:

audacter	boldly	**celeriter**	quickly
prudenter	wisely		

Position

- An adverb comes before the verb, adjective, adverb or noun that it modifies (→**1**)

- However adverbs of time often come at the beginning of the sentence (→**2**)

Continued

1   **vehementer** errabas, Verres
you were making a big mistake, Verres

    nimium libera respublica
too free a state

    bis consul
twice consul

2   **cras mane** putat se venturum esse
He thinks he will come tomorrow morning

    saepe hoc mecum cogitavi
I often thought this over by myself

Common Adverbs

- **Manner** – "how?"

ita	thus	**crudeliter**	cruelly
sīc	thus	**iustē**	justly
aliter	otherwise	**liberē**	freely
fortē	by chance	**repentē**	suddenly
magnoperē	greatly		

- **Time** – "when?"

iam, nunc	now	**(n)umquam**	(n)ever
simul	at the same time	**iterum**	again
anteā	before	**saepe**	often
posteā	afterwards	**hodiē**	today
cōtīdiē	every day	**herī**	yesterday
diū	for a long time	**crās**	tomorrow
mox	soon	**postrīdiē**	next day
interim *or* **-ea**	meanwhile	**statim**	immediately
tum	then		

● **Place** – "where?"

ubi?	where?	**unde?**	where from	**quō?**	where to?
ibi	there	**inde**	from there	**eō**	to there
hīc	here	**hinc**	from here	**hūc**	to here
usquam	anywhere	**nusquam**	nowhere		

Others

etiam	also	**fortasse**	perhaps
quoque	also	**consultō**	on purpose
quidem	indeed	**scīlicet**	no doubt

Comparison of Adverbs

The comparative form of the adverb is the nominative singular neuter of the comparative adjective. The superlative of the adverb is formed by changing -**us** of the superlative adjective to -**e**.

POSITIVE	COMPARATIVE	SUPERLATIVE
altē highly	**altius** more highly	**altissimē** most highly
audacter boldly	**audacius** more boldly	**audacissimē** most boldly
bene well	**melius** better	**optimē** best
breviter briefly	**brevius** more briefly	**brevissimē** most briefly
diū for a long time	**diūtius** longer	**diūtissimē** longest
facile easily	**facilius** more easily	**facillimē** most easily
magnoperē greatly	**magis** more	**maximē** most
male badly	**peius** worse	**pessimē** worst
miserē wretchedly	**miserius** more wretchedly	**miserrimē** most wretchedly
multum much	**plūs** more	**plūrimum** most
paulum a little	**minus** less	**minimē** least
prope near	**propius** nearer	**proxime** nearest
saepe often	**saepius** more often	**saepissimē** most often

● Notes on use of the comparative adjective may be applied also to the comparative adverb (*see p* 40).

rem totam brevius cognoscite
Find out about the whole matter more briefly

magis consilio quam virtute vicit
He won more because of his strategy than his courage

legiones diutius sine consule fuerunt
The legions were too long without a consul

multo plus
much more

optime
very well

mihi placebat Pomponius maxime vel minime
I liked Pomponius the most or disliked him the least

optimus quisque id optime facit
All the best people do it best

quam celerrime   as quickly as possible

Pronouns

Personal Pronouns

The pronouns **ego** (I), **nōs** (we), **tū** (you, *sing*), **vōs** (you, *pl*) decline as follows:

	SINGULAR			
Nom	**ego**	I	**tū**	you
Acc	**mē**	me	**tē**	you
Gen	**meī**	of me	**tuī**	of you
Dat	**mihi**	to/for me	**tibi**	to/for you
Abl	**mē**	by/with/ from me	**tē**	by/with/from you

	PLURAL			
Nom	**nōs**	we	**vōs**	you
Acc	**nōs**	us	**vōs**	you
Gen	**nostrum**	of us	**vestrum**	of you
Dat	**nōbis**	to/for us	**vobis**	to/for you
Abl	**nōbis**	by/with/ from us	**vōbis**	by/with/from you

Possessive

meus, -a, -um	my	**tuus, -a, -um**	your
noster, -ra, -rum	our	**vester, -ra, -rum**	your

- **nostri** and **vestri** are alternative forms of genitive plural.

- Possessives are sometimes used instead of the genitive of personal pronouns:

  odium tuum
  hatred of you

- For the third person pronoun, he/she/it, Latin uses **is**, **ea**, **id**:

SINGULAR

	Masc		Fem		Neut	
Nom	**is**	he	**ea**	she	**id**	it
Acc	**eum**	him	**eam**	her	**id**	it
Gen	**ēius**	of him	**ēius**	of her	**ēius**	of it
Dat	**eī**	to him	**eī**	to her	**eī**	to it
Abl	**eō**	by him	**eā**	by her	**eō**	by it

PLURAL

	Masc		Fem		Neut	
Nom	**eī**	they	**eae**	they	**ea**	they
Acc	**eōs**	them	**eās**	them	**ea**	them
Gen	**eōrum**	of them	**eārum**	of them	**eōrum**	of them
Dat	**eīs**	to them	**eīs**	to them	**eīs**	to them
Abl	**eīs**	by them	**eīs**	by them	**eīs**	by them

Use

- Pronouns as subjects (I, you) are not usually used in Latin. The person of the verb is indicated by the ending (*eg* **mīsimus** – we sent). **ego, nos** *etc* are used only for emphasis:

  ego vulgus odi, **tū** amas
  I hate crowds, you love them

- The genitive forms **nostrum** and **vestrum** are used partitively:

  multi **nostrum**
  many of us

  pauci **vestrum**
  a few of you

Reflexive Pronouns

Acc	**mē**	myself	**tē**	yourself
Gen	**meī**		**tuī**	
Dat	**mihi**		**tibi**	
Abl	**mē**		**tē**	
Acc	**nōs**	ourselves	**vōs**	yourselves
Gen	**nostrum**		**vestrum**	
Dat	**nōbis**		**vōbis**	
Abl	**nōbis**		**vōbis**	

- These are identical in form to personal pronouns.

Acc	**sē**	himself/herself/itself/themselves
Gen	**suī**	
Dat	**sibi**	
Abl	**sē**	

- Reflexive pronouns are used to refer to the subject of the sentence:

  quisque **se** amat
  everybody loves themselves

  me lavo
  I wash myself

Determinative Pronouns

- **is** – he/that, **ea** – she, **id** – it: as above
- **idem** (the same)

SINGULAR

	Masc	Fem	Neut
Nom	**īdem**	**eadem**	**idem**
Acc	**eundem**	**eandem**	**idem**
Gen	**ēiusdem**	**eīusdem**	**eīusdem**
Dat	**eīdem**	**eīdem**	**eīdem**
Abl	**eōdem**	**eadem**	**eōdem**

PLURAL

	Masc	Fem	Neut
Nom	**eīdem**	**eaedem**	**eadem**
Acc	**eōsdem**	**eāsdem**	**eadem**
Gen	**eōrundem**	**eārundem**	**eōrundem**
Dat	**eīsdem**	**eīsdem**	**eīsdem**
Abl	**eīsdem**	**eīsdem**	**eīsdem**

- **ipse** (himself/herself/itself/themselves)

SINGULAR

	Masc	Fem	Neut
Nom	**ipse**	**ipsa**	**ipsum**
Acc	**ipsum**	**ipsam**	**ipsum**
Gen	**ipsīus**	**ipsīus**	**ipsīus**
Dat	**ipsī**	**ipsī**	**ipsī**
Abl	**ipsō**	**ipsā**	**ipsō**

PLURAL

	Masc	Fem	Neut
Nom	**ipsī**	**ipsae**	**ipsa**
Acc	**ipsōs**	**ipsās**	**ipsa**
Gen	**ipsōrum**	**ipsārum**	**ipsōrum**
Dat	**ipsīs**	**ipsīs**	**ipsīs**
Abl	**ipsīs**	**ipsīs**	**ipsīs**

Demonstrative Pronouns

- **hic** (this/these)

	Masc	*SINGULAR* Fem	Neut
Nom	**hīc**	**haec**	**hōc**
Acc	**hunc**	**hanc**	**hōc**
Gen	**hūius**	**hūius**	**hūius**
Dat	**huīc**	**huīc**	**huīc**
Abl	**hōc**	**hāc**	**hōc**

	PLURAL		
Nom	**hī**	**hae**	**haec**
Acc	**hōs**	**hās**	**haec**
Gen	**hōrum**	**hārum**	**hōrum**
Dat	**hīs**	**hīs**	**hīs**
Abl	**hīs**	**hīs**	**hīs**

- **ille** (that/those)

	Masc	*SINGULAR* Fem	Neut
Nom	**ille**	**illa**	**illud**
Acc	**illum**	**illam**	**illud**
Gen	**illīus**	**illīus**	**illīus**
Dat	**illī**	**illī**	**illī**
Abl	**illō**	**illā**	**illō**

	PLURAL		
Nom	**illī**	**illae**	**illa**
Acc	**illōs**	**illās**	**illa**
Gen	**illōrum**	**illārum**	**illōrum**
Dat	**illīs**	**illīs**	**illīs**
Abl	**illīs**	**illīs**	**illīs**

- Note that **īdem**, **hīc**, **ille** and all their parts may be adjectives as well as pronouns

1   **eadem** femina
the same woman

hic puer
this boy

tu autem **eadem** ages?
Are you going to do the same things?

2   patria est carior quam **nos ipsi**
Our native land is dearer than ourselves

3   **hac** remota, quomodo **illum** aestimemus?
When she is removed, how are we to judge him?

4   **nos** oportet opus conficere
We must complete the task

5   accusatores dicunt **te ipsam** testem **eius** criminis esse
The prosecutors claim that you yourself are the witness
of that crime

6   sed **haec** omitto; ad **illa** quae **me** magis moverunt
respondeo
But I pass over these matters; I reply to those which
have affected me more deeply

7   pax **vobis**cum
Peace be with you!

8   puella intravit; **ea mihi** litteras dedit
The girl came in; she gave me a letter

Relative Pronouns

SINGULAR

	Masc		Fem	
Nom	**quī**	who	**quae**	who
Acc	**quem**	whom	**quam**	whom
Gen	**cūius**	whose	**cūius**	whose
Dat	**cuī**	to whom	**cuī**	to whom
Abl	**quō**	by whom	**quā**	by whom

	Neut	
Nom	**quod**	which/that
Acc	**quod**	which/that
Gen	**cūius**	of which
Dat	**cuī**	to which
Abl	**quō**	by which

PLURAL

	Masc		Fem	
Nom	**quī**	who	**quae**	who
Acc	**quōs**	whom	**quās**	whom
Gen	**quōrum**	whose	**quārum**	whose
Dat	**quibus**	to whom	**quibus**	to whom
Abl	**quibus**	by whom	**quibus**	by whom

	Neut	
Nom	**quae**	which
Acc	**quae**	which
Gen	**quōrum**	of which
Dat	**quibus**	to which
Abl	**quibus**	by which

- A relative pronoun attaches a subordinate clause to a word preceding it (its antecedent). It agrees with this word in number and gender but takes its case from its own clause (→**1**)

- **quidam**, **quaedam**, **quoddam** (a certain, somebody) **quīcumque**, **quaecumque**, **quodcumque** (whoever/ whatever), decline in the same way as the relative above (→**2**)

1   iuvenis cuius librum Sextus legit laetus erat
The young man, whose book Sextus read, was happy

Fortunata, quae erat uxor Trimalchionis, saltare coeperat
Fortunata, who was Trimalchio's wife, had begun to dance

tum duo crotalia protulit quae Fortunatae consideranda dedit
Then she brought out a pair of earrings which she gave to Fortunata to look at

2   quidam ex legatis
a certain ambassador

tu, **quicumque** es
you, whoever you are

Interrogative Pronouns

SINGULAR

	Masc		Fem	
Nom	**quis**	who?	**quis/quae**	who?
Acc	**quem**	whom?	**quam**	whom?
Gen	**cūius**	whose?	**cūius**	whose?
Dat	**cuī**	to whom?	**cuī**	to whom?
Abl	**quō**	by whom?	**quā**	by whom?

	Neut				
Nom	**quid**	what?	Dat	**cuī**	to what?
Acc	**quid**	what?	Abl	**quō**	by what?
Gen	**cūius**	of what?			

PLURAL

	Masc		Fem	
Nom	**quī**	who?	**quae**	who?
Acc	**quōs**	whom?	**quās**	whom?
Gen	**quōrum**	whose?	**quārum**	whose?
Dat	**quibus**	towhom?	**quibus**	to whom?
Abl	**quibus**	by whom?	**quibus**	by whom?

	Neut				
Nom	**quae**	what?	Dat	**quibus**	to what?
Acc	**quae**	what?	Abl	**quibus**	by what?
Gen	**quōrum**	of what?			

- The interrogative pronoun is used to ask questions and usually is the first word in the sentence (→**1**)

- **quisquis, quisquis, quidquid** (whoever, whatever)
  quisque, quisque, quidque (each)
  quisquam, quisquam, quicquam (anyone, anything)
  aliquis, aliquis, aliquid (someone, something)
  These pronouns decline in the same way as **quis** above
  (→**2**)

1 **quae fuit enim causa quamobrem isti mulieri venenum dare vellet Caelius?**
What was the reason why Caelius wanted to give that woman poison?

quid agam, iudices?
What am I to do, men of the jury?

quos ad cenam invitavisti?
Whom did you invite for dinner?

quorum agros Galli incenderunt?
Whose fields did the Gauls burn?

2 **quisque** is est
whoever he is

si **quemquam** video
if I see anyone

liber **alicuius**
someone's book

Prepositions

A preposition expresses the relationship of one word to another. Each Latin preposition governs a noun or pronoun in the accusative or ablative case. Some prepositions govern both cases. Some may also be used as adverbs *eg* **prope** (near).

Position

- Prepositions generally come before the noun, or an adjective or equivalent qualifying the noun *eg*

  ad villam
  to the house

  ad Ciceronis villam
  to Cicero's house

- **cum** follows a personal pronoun *eg*

  mēcum
  with me

Prepositions governing the Accusative

On the following pages you will find some of the most frequent uses of prepositions in Latin. In the list below, the broad meaning is given on the left, with examples of usage following. Prepositions are given in alphabetical order.

ad

to/towards (*a place or person*)	**oculos ad caelum sustulit** he raised his eyes to heaven
at, in the direction of, with regard to	**ad Capuam profectus sum** I set out in the direction of Capua
	ad portas at the gates
	ad duo milia occisi about 2000 were killed
	nil ad me attinet it means nothing to me

adversum (-us)

opposite	**sedens adversus te** sitting opposite you
towards	**adversus Italiam** towards (*ie* facing) Italy
against	**adversum flumen** against the stream

Continued

Prepositions governing the Accusative (contd)

ante

before (*of place and time*), used with ordinal number in dates

ante meridiem
before midday

ante limen
before the doorway

ante diem quintum Kalendas Ianuarias
28th December (*ie* 5th before Kalends of January)

apud

at/near (*usually with persons*)

Crassus apud eum sedet
Crassus is sitting near him

in the writing of

apud Platonem
in Plato's writings

before (*authorities*)

apud pontifices
before the high priests

circum (circa)

around, about (*of place, people*)

circum forum
around the forum

circum Hectorem
around Hector

circa montes
around the mountains

circa decem milia Gallorum
about ten thousand Gauls

contra

against
    contra hostes
    against the enemy

    contra ventos
    against the wind

opposite
    contra Britanniam
    facing Britain

extra

outside of
    extra muros
    outside the walls

beyond (*of place and time*)
    extra iocum
    beyond a joke

inter

between
    inter oppositos exercitus
    between the opposing
    armies

    amans inter se
    loving each other

among
    inter saucios
    among the wounded

    inter manus
    within reach

during
    inter hos annos
    during these years

Continued

Prepositions governing the Accusative
(contd)

intra

within (*of place and time*)   **intra parietes**
within the walls

intra quattuor annos
within four years

ob

on account of   **quam ob rem**
therefore

ob stultitiam
on account of your
foolishness

per

through   **per noctem**
through the night

by means of   **per vos**
by means of you

per aetatem periit
he died of old age

per deos iuro
I swear by the gods

post

after (*of time and place*)

post urbem conditam
after the foundation of the city

post tergum
behind your back

praeter

beyond

praeter naturam
beyond nature

besides

praeter se tres alios adduxit
he brought three others besides himself

except for

praeter paucos
except for a few

prope

near

prope me habitavit
he lived near me

propter

on account of

propter metum mortis
on account of fear of death

Continued

Prepositions governing the Accusative
(contd)

secundum

along (*of place*)	**secundum flumen** along the river
immediately after (*time*)	**secundum quietem** on waking from sleep
according to	**secundum naturam** according to nature

trans

across	**vexillum trans vallum traicere** to take the standard across the rampart
	trans Rhenum across the Rhine

ultra

beyond (*of time, degree etc*)	**ultra vires** beyond one's power

Prepositions governing the Ablative

Those which are spatial represent the idea of rest **in** a place or motion **from** a place.

a(b)

from (*of place, people, direction, time*)

ab arce hostes deiecti sunt
the enemy were driven from the citadel

a nobis abesse
to be distant from us

a dextrā
from the right

a tertiā horā
from the third hour

by (*agent*)

ab amicis desertus
abandoned by friends

cum

with

vade mecum
go with me!

cum curā loqui
to speak with care

cum Augusto coniurare
to conspire with Augustus

summa cum laude
with distinction

Continued

Prepositions governing the Ablative
(contd)

dē

down from	**dē caelō demittere** to send down from heaven
away from	**de tricliniō exire** to go away from the dining room
about	**cogitare de hāc rē** to think about this matter
	dē industriā on purpose
during *or* at (*of time*)	**dē nocte** at night, during the night

ē(x)

out of (*from*)	**ē carcere effugerunt** they escaped from prison
	ex equis desilire to jump from their horses
	quidam ex Hispania someone from Spain
	statua ex argentō facta a statue made of silver
immediately after	**ex consulatu** immediately after his consulship
from	**ex hōc diē** from that day
	ex aequō equally

pro

for/on behalf of	**pro se quisque** each one for himself/herself
	pro patriā morī to die for one's country
according to	**pro viribus agere** to act according to one's ability
in front of	**pro rostris** in front of the rostrum

sine

without	**sine spē** without hope
	sine pecuniā without money

Prepositions governing Accusative and Ablative

in

with accusative

into
in hanc urbem venire
to come into the city

till
in primam lucem dormivit
he slept till dawn

against
in rem publicam aggredi
to attack the state

with ablative

in
puella in illā domō laetē vivebat
the girl lived happily in that house

on
in capite coronam gerebat
he wore a crown on his head

in animo habere
to intend (to have in one's mind)

within (*of time*)
in omni aetate
within every age

in (*of condition*)
in parte facilis, in parte difficilis
easy in parts, difficult in others

sub

with accusative

beneath

sub iugum mittere
to send beneath the yoke
(*ie* into slavery)

below (*with verb of motion*)

sub ipsum murum
just below the wall

before (*of time*)

sub vesperum
just before nightfall

with ablative

under (*of place and power*)

sub montibus constituere
to station under the mountains

sub Nerone
under the power of Nero

super

with accusative

over, above (*of place*), in addition

super capita hostium
over the heads of the enemy

alii, super alios, advenerunt
they arrived one after the other

with ablative

concerning/about

super his rebus scribam
I shall write about these matters

Numerals

Cardinal and Ordinal Numbers

		CARDINAL	ORDINAL
1	I	ūnus, -a,-um	prīmus, -a, -um
2	II	duo, -ae, -o	secundus, -a, -um
3	III	trēs, tria	tertius, -a, -um
4	IV	quattuor	quartus, -a, -um
5	V	quīnque	quīntus, -a, -um
6	VI	sex	sextus, -a, -um
7	VII	septem	septimus, -a, -um
8	VIII	octō	octāvus, -a, -um
9	IX	novem	nōnus, -a, -um
10	X	decem	decimus, -a, -um
11	XI	ūndecim	ūndecimus, -a, -um
12	XII	duodecim	duodecimus, -a, -um
13	XIII	tredecim	tertius decimus, -a, -um
14	XIV	quattuordecim	quartus decimus, -a, -um
15	XV	quīndecim	quintus decimus, -a, -um
16	XVI	sēdecim	sextus decimus, -a, -um
17	XVII	septendecim	septimus decimus, -a, -um
18	XVIII	duodēvigintī	duodēvicēsimus, -a, -um
19	XIX	ūndēvigintī	undēvicēsimus, -a, -um
20	XX	vigintī	vicēsimus, -a, -um
21	XXI	vigintī ūnus	vicēsimus prīmus
30	XXX	trīgintā	trīcēsimus
40	XL	quadrāgintā	quadrāgēsimus
50	L	quīnquāgintā	quīnquāgēsimus
60	LX	sexāgintā	sexāgēsimus
70	LXX	septuāgintā	septuāgēsimus
80	LXXX	octōgintā	octōgēsimus
90	XC	nōnāgintā	nōnāgēsimus
100	C	centum	centēsimus

		CARDINAL	ORDINAL
200	**CC**	ducentī, -ae, -a	ducentēsimus
300	**CCC**	trecentī, -ae, -a	trecentēsimus
400	**CCCC**	quadringentī, -ae, -a	quadringentēsimus
500	**D (IϽ)**	quīngentī, -ae, -a	quīngentēsimus
600	**DC**	sescentī, -ae, -a	sescentēsimus
700	**DCC**	septingentī, -ae, -a	septingentēsimus
800	**DCCC**	octingentī, -ae, -a	octingentēsimus
900	**DCCCC**	nōngentī, -ae, -a	nōngentēsimus
1000 M (CIϽ)		mīlle	mīllēsimus
2000 MM		duo mīlia	bis mīllēsimus
1,000,000		deciēs centēna (centum)	mīlia

- Fractions are expressed as follows:
  dimidia pars 1/2
  tertia pars 1/3
  quārta pars 1/4

Continued

Cardinal and Ordinal Numbers (contd)

- Ordinal numbers (→1) decline like 1st and 2nd declension adjectives

- Cardinal numbers (→2) do not decline except for **ūnus**, **duo**, **trēs** and hundreds (**ducenti** etc)

- **unus** declines as 1st and 2nd declension adjectives except that the genitive singular ends in -**ius** and the dative in -**i**

- **duo** (two) declines as follows:

	Masc	Fem	Neut
Nom	**duo**	**duae**	**duo**
Acc	**duōs**	**duās**	**duo**
Gen	**duōrum**	**duārum**	**duōrum**
Dat	**duōbus**	**duābus**	**duōbus**
Abl	**duōbus**	**duābus**	**duōbus**

ambō, -ae, -a (both) declines in the same way

- **trēs** (three) declines as follows:

	Masc	Fem	Neut
Nom	**trēs**	**trēs**	**tria**
Acc	**trēs**	**trēs**	**tria**
Gen	**trium**	**trium**	**trium**
Dat	**tribus**	**tribus**	**tribus**
Abl	**tribus**	**tribus**	**tribus**

- Genitive of hundreds, eg **trecentī** ends -**um** (→3)

- **mīlia** (thousands) declines as follows:

Nom	**mīlia**	Dat	**mīlibus**
Acc	**mīlia**	Abl	**mīlibus**
Gen	**mīlium**		

- **mīlle** (thousand) does not decline.

1 coquus **secundam** mensam paraverat
The cook had prepared the second course

legionis **nonae** milites magnam partem hostium interfecerunt
Soldiers of the ninth legion killed a large number of the enemy

2 **decem milia** passuum exercitus progressus est
The army advanced 10 miles

Cerberus, qui **tria** capita habebat, in antro recubuit
Cerberus, who had three heads, crouched in the cave

Stellae **novem** orbes confecerunt
The stars completed nine orbits

duodeviginti onerariae naves huc accedebant
Eighteen cargo ships were approaching

Caesar **trecentos** milites trans Padanum traiecit
Caesar transported three hundred soldiers across the River Po

da mi basia **mille**
Give me a thousand kisses

3 **trecentum militum**
of three hundred soldiers

4 **duo milia passuum** (*gen*)
2000 paces *or* 2 miles

Distributive Numerals

These are used when repetition is involved as when multiplying (→**1**)

1	**singulī, -ae, -a**	*one each*
2	**bīnī, -ae, -a**	*two each*
3	**ternī (trinī)**	
4	**quaternī**	
5	**quīnī**	
6	**sēnī**	
7	**septēnī**	
8	**octōnī**	
9	**novēnī**	
10	**dēni**	

Numeral Adverbs

1	**semel**	*once*
2	**bis**	*twice*
3	**ter**	
4	**quater**	
5	**quīnquiēs**	
6	**sexiēs**	
7	**septiēs**	
8	**octiēs**	
9	**noviēs**	
10	**deciēs**	

(→**2**)

1 **bini** gladiatores
   (*describing pairs of gladiators*)

   bina castra
   two camps

   quaternos denarios in **singulas** vini amphoras
   4 denarii each for a bottle of wine

2 non plus quam **semel**
   not more than once

   decies centena milia sestertium *or* **decies** sestertium
   1,000,000 sesterces

   ter quattuor
   twelve (*three times four*)

Dates

- Events of the year were usually recorded by using the names of the consuls holding office that year (→**1**)
- From the late republic the date of the foundation of Rome was established – 753 BC and time was calculated from this date (→**2**)
- The four seasons were: (→**3**)

  ver, veris (*nt*)   spring
  aestās, -atis (*f*)   summer
  autumnus, -i (*m*)   autumn
  hiems, -is (*f*)   winter

- The months were reformed by Julius Caesar (7 of 31 days, 4 of 30, 1 of 28, and an extra day each leap year). Each month (**mensis**, -**is**, *m*) was identified by the following adjectives:

  Iānuārius   January
  Februārius   February
  Martius   March
  Āprīlis   April
  Māius   May
  Iūnius   June
  Iulīus (Quintīlis)   July
  Augustus (Sextīlis)   August
  September   September
  Octōber   October
  November   November
  December   December

- Three important days each month were:

  Kalendae, -arum (*fpl*)   Kalends *or* 1st
  Nonae, -arum (*fpl*)   Nones *or* 5th/7th
  Idus, -uum (*fpl*)   Ides *or* 13th/15th

Continued

1 Nerone iterum L. Pisone consulibus pauca memoria
    digna evenerunt
    Few incidents worth recording took place during the
    year when Nero and Lucius Piso were consuls (AD 57)

 Lentulo Gaetulico C. Calvisio consulibus decreta sunt
 triumphi insignia Poppaeo Sabino
 A triumph was voted to Poppaeus Sabinus during the
 consulship of Lentulus Gaetulicius and Gaius Calvisius

2 ab urbe condita
 since the foundation of Rome

 ante urbem conditam
 before the foundation of the city

 post urbem conditam
 after the foundation of the city

3 ineunte aestate
 in the beginning of summer

 media **aestate**
 midsummer

 iam **hieme confecta**
 when winter was already over

 vere ineunte Antonius Tarentum navigavit
 At the beginning of spring, Antony sailed to Tarentum

Dates (contd)

- In March, July, October and May, Nones fall on the 7th and Ides on the 15th day (5th and 13th in all other months).

- To refer to these dates, the ablative is used (→**1**)

- To refer to the day before these dates, use **pridiē** (→**2**)

- All other days were reckoned by counting (inclusively) the days before the next main date. "ante diem" + accusative of ordinal numbers and the next main date were used:
  9th of February is 5 days before the 13th of February (counting inclusively). 28th April is 4 days before 1st May (→**3**)

- An easy way to work out such dates is to add one to Nones and Ides and subtract the Latin number. Add two to the number of days in the month before the Kalends, again subtracting the given Latin number. You will then have the date in English.

- The day was divided into twelve hours **horae, -arum** (*fpl*). The hours of darkness into four watches of three hours each, **vīgiliae, -arum** (*fpl*), from 6–9 pm, 9–12 pm, 12–3 am, 3–6 am

- Other ways of expressing time:

primā luce	at dawn
sole orto	at sunrise
solis occasu	at sunset
media nocte	at midnight
noctu, nocte	at night
mane	in the morning
meridie	at midday
sub vesperum	towards evening
vespere	in the evening (→**4**)

1 **Kalendīs Martiis**
   on the 1st of March

   Idibus Decembribus
   on the 13th of December

   Idibus Martiis Caesar a Bruto interfectus est
   Caesar was killed by Brutus on the 15th of March

2 **pridie Nonas Ianuarias (Non. Ian.)**
   4th January

3 **ante diem quintum Idus Februarias**
   9th February

   ante diem quartum Kalendas Maias
   28th April

4 **prima hora**
   at the first hour (6–7 am)

   tertia vigilia
   during the third watch (midnight–3 am)

   tertia fere vigilia navem solvit
   He set sail after midnight (during the third watch)

   ipse **hora circiter quarta diei** cum primis navibus
   Britanniam attigit
   He himself reached Britain with the first ships around
   10 o'clock in the morning

   vespere vinum optimum convivae bibunt
   In the evening, the guests drink vintage wine

Word Order

Simple Sentences

Word order in English is stricter than in Latin. The usual English order – subject + verb + object – differentiates the meaning of sentences such as, "The cat caught the mouse" and "The mouse caught the cat". Latin order is more flexible since the endings of words clearly show their function, whatever their position in the sentence.

Compare the following:

feles murem cepit the cat caught the mouse
murem cepit feles it was the cat that caught the mouse

The sentences are identical in meaning, although the emphasis is different. This difference in word order often makes it difficult for English translators to unravel long Latin sentences. However there are certain principles to help:

● The normal *grammatical* word order in Latin is:

Subject first, Predicate after (by Predicate understand "verb")

● Expressions qualifying the subject (*ie* adjectives) must be near the subject

● Expressions qualifying the predicate (*eg* objects, adverbs, prepositional phrases) must be near the verb

Thus the usual word order of a simple sentence is:

(Connecting Word)
Subject
(Adjective)
Object
Adverbs *or* Prepositional Phrases
Predicate (verb) (→**1**)

Continued

1 at **hostes** magnam virtutem in extrema spe salutis **praestiterunt**
But the enemy showed great courage, finally hoping to save themselves

Ariovistus ad postulata Caesaris pauca **respondit**
Ariovistus briefly replied to Caesar's demands

iste **Hannibal** sic hanc Tertiam **dilexit**
Thus that Hannibal loved this Tertia

Simple Sentences (contd)

- Another principle is *emphasis*, where the words are in an unusual order, *eg* subject last, predicate first (→**1**)
- Questions usually begin with interrogatives (→**2**)
- Adjectives may precede or follow nouns. Check agreement of endings (→**3**)
- Genitives usually follow the governing word (→**4**)
- Words in apposition usually follow one another, although "rex" often comes first (→**5**)
- Adverbs usually come before their verb, adjective or adverb (→**6**)
- Prepositions usually come before their nouns (→**7**) but note, magna **cum** cura (with great care).
- Finally, watch out for the omission of words, particularly parts of **esse** (to be) (→**8**)

1 horum adventu **redintegratur** | **seditio** (subject last)
On their arrival trouble broke out once more

confecerunt me | **infirmitates** meorum (verb first)
I have been upset by the illnesses of my slaves

2 **quid** hoc loco potes dicere, homo amentissime?
What can you say at this point, you madman?

quis clarior in Graecia Themistocle?
Who (is) more famous in Greece than Themistocles?

3 **bello magno** victus   **magna domus**
conquered in a great war   a large house

4 multi **nostrum**   filius **Augusti**
many of us   Augustus' son

5 Cicero, **consul**
Cicero, the consul

rex Tarquinius
King Tarquinius

6 **vix** cuiquam persuadebatur
hardly anyone could be persuaded

multo carius
much dearer

7 **in** villam
into the house

sub monte
under the mountain

8 **pudor inde et miseratio et patris Agrippae, Augusti avi memoria (est)**
A feeling of pity and shame came over them and they remembered her father Agrippa and her grandfather Augustus

Compound Sentences

A compound sentence is one with a main clause and one or more subordinate clauses. In Latin this is called a **period**, where the most important idea is kept to the end.

- conservate parenti filium, parentem filio, (1) ne aut senectutem iam prope desperatam contempsisse aut adulescentiam plenam spei｜maximae non modo non aluisse vos verum etiam perculisse atque adflixisse videamini (2). (Cic. – Pro Caelio 32.80)

  1. Main clause
     save a son for his father, a father for his son.
  2. Negative purpose clause
     lest you appear either to have cast aside an old man near despair or that you have failed to sustain a young man full of the highest hopes, but have even struck him down and ruined him.

  Note that this sentence builds towards a climax at the end. The most important verbs here are **perculisse** and **adflixisse** rather than **videamini** (you may seem). Notice also the rhythm of the last two words. Repetition of similar phrases is common – **parenti filium**, **parentem filio**. This sentence is a good illustration of an orator's style.

- Historical style is much simpler, often a subordinate clause followed by a main clause:

  cum equites nostri funditoribus sagittariisque flumen transgressi essent (1), cum equitatu proelium commiserunt

1. Subordinate adverbial clause of time
   when our cavalry had crossed the river with slingers and archers
2. Main clause
   they joined battle with the cavalry

- Participle phrase followed by the **main clause** and **subordinate** clause:

nec patrum cognitionibus satiatus iudiciis (1), adsidebat in cornu tribunalis (2), ne praetorem curuli depelleret (Tac Ann I 75)

1. Participle phrase
   nor was he (the emperor) satisfied with taking part in Senate trials
2. Main clause
   he used to sit in the ordinary lawcourts
3. Subordinate clause of purpose
   in case he pushed the praetor from his curule chair

Many other combinations of clauses are possible. It is important to relate the sentence to its context and to the passage as a whole as Latin sentences are linked logically. It is often helpful when translating a long sentence to pick out subjects and verbs in order to recognize the structure of the clauses and grasp the overall meaning of the sentence.

Simple Sentences

Direct Statement

The basic patterns involved in direct statement have been illustrated under **Word Order** (*see* p 80).

Direct Questions

In Latin a direct question can be expressed as follows by:

- an interrogative pronoun (→**1**)

    quis? (who?), **quid**? (what?), **cur**? (why?)

- adding **-ne** to the first word, where no definite answer is indicated (→**2**)

- **nonne**, when the expected answer is YES (→**3**)

- **num**, when the expected answer is NO (→**4**)

- **utrum** … **an(non)**
  -ne …**an(non)** } (whether) … or (not)
  … **an(non)**
  in double questions (→**5**)

Continued

1   **quis** est
Who is it?

        quid dicit?
What is he saying?

        cur lacrimas?
Why are you crying?

2   times**ne** Verrem?
Are you scared of Verres?

3   **nonne** cladem audivisti?
Surely you heard of the defeat?
   or You heard of the defeat, didn't you?

4   **num** heri venisti?
Surely you didn't come yesterday?
   or You didn't come yesterday, did you?

5   utrum has condiciones accepistis **annon**?
Have you accepted these conditions or not?

Simple Sentences (contd)

Direct Command

- A direct command in Latin is expressed in the second person by the imperative if positive, by **nolī(te)** with the present infinitive if negative (→**1**)

- A direct command in the first or third persons is expressed by the present subjunctive, with **nē** if negative (→**2**)

Wishes

- Wishes are expressed in Latin by **utinam** with the subjunctive, **utinam nē** when negative (→**3**)

- **vellem** may also be used with imperfect or pluperfect subjunctive to express wishes (→**4**)

1   **venite** mecum
come with me

   noli me tangere
don't touch me

2   **vivamus** atque **amemus**
let us live and let us love

   ne **fiat** lux
let there not be light

3   **utinam** frater redeat
I wish my brother would return (*future*)

   utinam ne vere scriberem
I wish I were not writing the truth (*present*)

   utinam brevi moratus esses
I wish you had stayed a little (*past*)

4   **vellem** me ad cenam **invitavisses**
I wish you had invited me to dinner

Compound Sentences

Indirect Statement

"You are making a mistake" is a *direct statement*. "I think that you are making a mistake" is an *indirect statement*.

- The indirect statement is the object clause of "I think". In indirect statement in Latin, the subject of the clause (*eg* te) goes into the accusative case, the verb is an infinitive (errare):

  Puto **te errare**
  I think that you are making a mistake

- This pattern is used after verbs of saying, thinking, perceiving, knowing (→**1**)

Continued

1

audire	hear	**negare**	say … not
cognoscere	discover	**nescire**	not to know
credere	believe	**putare**	think
dicere	say	**scire**	know
intellegere	understand	**sentire**	perceive
meminisse	remember	**videre**	see
narrare	tell		

Indirect Statement (contd)

Translation

- The *present infinitive* refers to actions happening at the same time and may be translated – is, are, was, were.

- The *perfect infinitive* refers to prior action and may be translated – has, have, had.

- The *future infinitive* refers to future action and may be translated – will, would.

putamus	**te errāre**
	te errāvisse
	te errātūrum esse
We think	that you are making a mistake
	that you have made a mistake
	that you will make a mistake

putabamus	**te errāre**
	te errāvisse
	te errātūrum esse
We thought	that you were making a mistake
	that you had made a mistake
	that you would make a mistake

- Notice that when the main verb is *past* tense, translate the present infinitive – "was, were", the past infinitive – "had", the future infinitive – "would".

- The reflexive pronoun **sē** is used to refer to the subject of the main verb (→**1**)

- Translate **negō** – I say that ... not (→**2**)

- Verbs of promising, hoping, threatening or swearing (*eg* **promitto**, **pollicēor**, **spērō**, **minor**, **iuro**) are followed by an accusative and future infinitive (→**3**)

1   senex dixit **se** thesaurum invenisse
      The old man said that he had found treasure

2   **negavit** servum domum venturum esse
      He said that the slave would not come home

3   **promisi me festinaturum esse**
      I promised that I would hurry

      sperabat se hoc confecturum esse
      He hoped that he could complete this
   or He hoped to complete this

Further Examples

creditores existimabant **eum** totam pecuniam **perdidisse**
His creditors thought that he had lost all his money

memini **simulacra** deorum de caelo **percussa esse**
I remember that the gods' statues were struck down from the heavens

vidistine **Catonem** in bibliotheca **sedere**?
Did you see Cato sitting in the library?

iuro **me** pro patria fortiter **pugnaturum esse**
I swear that I shall fight bravely for my country

iam ego credo **vos** verum **dixisse**
I now believe that you spoke the truth

negavit **nihil** umquam pulchrius statua **fuisse**
He said that nothing had ever been more beautiful than that statue

Indirect Question

"Where did he come from?" is a *direct question*. "I asked where he had come from" is an *indirect question*. Latin uses the same interrogative words (**quis** – who, **quid** – what *etc*) and the verb in indirect questions is always subjunctive

> rogavi **unde venisset**
> I asked where he had come from

● Latin uses six different forms of the subjunctive in this construction in a precise sequence depending on the main verb (→**1**)

1 rogo   **unde veniat**   (present)
           unde venerit   (perfect)
           unde venturus sit   (future)

    I ask   where he comes from   (present)
           where he has come from   (perfect)
           where he will come from   (future)

    rogavi   **unde veniret**   (imperfect)
           unde venisset   (pluperfect)
           unde venturus esset   (future perfect)

    I asked   where he was coming   (imperfect)
             from
           where he had come from   (pluperfect)
           where he would come   (future perfect)
             from

Indirect Question (contd)

Translation

Translation of tenses in indirect question is *easy*, because English uses the same tenses as Latin, as can be seen on page 94.

- The reflexive pronoun **se** is used to refer to the subject of the main verb (→**1**)

- **utrum** ... **an** (if ... or), **utrum** ... **necne** (whether ... or not) are also used in indirect questions (→**2**)

- **num** is used to mean "if" in indirect questions (→**3**)

1 rogavit **quando se visuri essemus**
   He asked when we would see him

2 roga **utrum** iverit **an** manserit
   Ask whether he went or stayed

   roga **utrum** manserit **necne**
   Ask whether he stayed or not

   rogavit **utrum** Scylla infestior **esset** Charybdis **necne**
   He asked whether Charybdis was more dangerous than
   Scylla or not

3 nescio **num** venturi sint
   I don't know if they will come

Further Examples

   nescimus **quid facturi simus**
   We don't know what we shall do

   mirum est **quanta sit Roma**
   It is amazing how big Rome is
   or The size of Rome is amazing

   exploratores cognoverunt **quanti essent** Poeni
   Scouts discovered what the numbers of the
   Carthaginians were

   incredibile est **quomodo** talia facere **potuerit**
   It is incredible how he was able to do such things

   nemo audivit **quid** rex **constituisset**
   No one heard what the king had decided
   or No one heard the king's decision

Indirect Command

"Come here" is a *direct command*. "I ordered you to come here" is an *indirect command*. Indirect commands in Latin are expressed by **ut** (when positive) or **nē** (when negative) and have their verbs in the subjunctive (→**1**)

● Latin uses two tenses of the subjunctive, present or imperfect, in this construction. It uses the present subjunctive if the main verb is present or future tense and imperfect subjunctive if the main verb is in the past tense. (→**2**)

Translation

● The English translation of the indirect command is the same, whichever tense is used in Latin – the infinitive (*eg* to come)

● The reflexive **se** is used to refer to the subject of the main verb (→**3**)

● Common verbs introducing indirect command are:

hortor	encourage
moneo	warn
oro	beg
persuadeo	persuade
rogo	ask

● *Only* **iubeo** (to order), **veto** (to tell … not), are usually used with the infinitive in Latin (→**4**)

1 tibi imperavi **ut venīrēs**
I ordered you to come

tibi imperavi **ne venires**
I forbade you to come

milites oravit **ne** in castris diutius **manerent**
He begged his soldiers not to stay in camp any longer

hoc rogo, mi Tiro, **ne** temere **naviges**
I beg you, my dear Tiro, not to sail carelessly

2 tibi **impero ut venias**   (*present*)
I order you to come

tibi **imperavi ut venires**   (*imperfect*)
I ordered you to come

deos precor **ut** nobis **parcant**
I beg the gods to spare us

amicos roga **ut veniant**, operamque **dent**, et messim
hanc nobis **adiuvent**
Ask your friends to come and lend a hand and help
us with this harvest

3 nos oravit ut **sibi** cibum daremus
He begged us to give him food

4 **iubeo** eos **navigare**
I order them to sail

veto eos **navigare**
I tell them not to sail

mater me **vetuit** in murum **ascendere**
Mother forbade me to climb on the wall

Antonius eos **iussit** adventum **suum exspectare**
Antony told them to await his arrival

Purpose or Final Clauses

There are two ways of expressing purpose in English:

> I am hurrying to the city to see the games
>
> *or* I am hurrying to the city so that I may see the games

- In Latin **ut** is used with the present or imperfect subjunctive, to express purpose. The present subjunctive is used if the main verb is in the present or future tense and the imperfect subjunctive if the main verb is in the past tense (→**1**)

- Negative purpose clauses are introduced by **ne** which can be translated "so that … not", "in case", "to avoid", "lest" etc (→**2**)

- If there is a comparative adjective or adverb in the Latin sentence **quō** is used instead of **ut** (→**3**)

- The relative **qui**, **quae**, **quod** may be used instead of **ut**, if it refers to an object in the main clause (→**4**)

- After negative **ne**, **quis** is used instead of **aliquis** to mean "anyone"

  Note that **se** is used to refer to the subject of the main verb (→**5**)

- **ad** is used with the gerundive to express purpose (→**6**)

- The supine -**um** is used after verbs of motion to express purpose (→**7**)

1 ad urbem festino **ut** ludos **videam**
I am hurrying to the city to see the games
ad urbem festinavi **ut** ludos **viderem**
I hurried to the city to see the games
filium multo cum fletu complexus, pepulit **ut abiret**
Embracing his son tearfully, he drove him to leave

2 Tiberius hoc recusavit **ne** Germanicus imperium **haberet**
Tiberius refused this lest Germanicus had power
pontem resciderunt **ne** hostes flumen **transirent**
They broke down the bridge in case the enemy crossed
the river

3 puellae cantabant **quo** laetiores essent **hospites**
The girls sang to make their guests happier

4 rex sex milites delegit **qui** ad Graeciam **proficiscerentur**
The king chose six soldiers to set off for Greece

5 in silvis se abdidit **ne quis se** videret
He hid in the woods lest anyone should see him
sed **ut** venenum manifesto comprehendi **posset**, constitui locum iussit, **ut** eo **mitteret** amicos, **qui laterent**,
cum venisset Licinius, venenumque traderet, comprehenderent
But *so that the poison could be seized openly*, he
ordered that a place be appointed, *to send friends
there, to hide*. When Licinius came to hand over the
poison they could arrest him.

6 Verres ad Siciliam venit **ad urbes diripiendas**
Verres came to Sicily to plunder its cities

7 veniunt **spectatum**
They come to see

Result or Consecutive Clauses

The road is so long that I am tired
It was so hot that we could not work

In both these sentences, a result or consequence is expressed in English by using words such as

so ... that (positive)
so that ... not (negative)

- In Latin the following words are frequently used in the main clause

adeo	to such an extent
ita	thus, so
talis	of such a kind
tam	so
tantus	so great
tot	so many

- In the result clause, **ut** (so that) and **ut ... non** (so that ... not) are used with the present or imperfect subjunctive. Present subjunctive is used where the main verb is in the present and the imperfect subjunctive is used where the main verb is past (→**1**)

- **Note** that **eum** is used to refer to "him" instead of **se** when referring to the subject of the main clause as in the first example (→**1**)

1   Gallus **tam** ferox est **ut** omnes Romani eum **timeant**
The Gaul is so fierce that all the Romans are scared
of him

tanta erat tempestas **ut** nautae navem **non solverent**
So great was the storm that the sailors could not set
sail

nemo est **adeo** stultus **ut non** discere **possit**
No one is so stupid that he can't learn

tot sententiae erant **ut nemo consentiret**
There were so many opinions that no one could
agree

tales nos esse putamus **ut** ab omnibus **laudemur**
We think that we are the sort of people to be praised
by everyone

Verbs of Fearing

In Latin, verbs of fearing (**timeo**, **metuo**, **paveo**, **vereor**) are followed by **nē**, **nē non** or **ut** with the present and perfect, imperfect and pluperfect subjunctive according to sequence of tenses:

- The present subjunctive represents present and future tenses in English

   I am afraid he is coming
   I am afraid he will come

- The perfect subjunctive represents the past tense in English

   I am afraid that he has come

- When the verb of fearing is in the past tense, imperfect and pluperfect subjunctive are used in Latin instead (→**1**)

- **nē** is used if the fear is expressed in a positive sentence (*ie* I am afraid he will come). **nē nōn**, **ut** is used if the fear is expressed negatively (*ie* I am afraid that he won't come) (→**2**)

- As in English, the infinitive can follow a verb of fearing, provided that the subjects of both are the same (→**3**)

1   veritus sum **ne veniret**
I was afraid he was coming

veritus sum **ne venisset**
I was afraid that he had come

2   **vereor ne** amicus **veniat**
I am afraid lest my friend comes
  or lest my friend will come

vereor ne amicus **non veniat**
I am afraid that my friend won't come

vereor ut amicus **venerit**
I am afraid that my friend has not come

verebar ne amicus **non venisset**
I was afraid that my friend had not come

metuo ne virtutis maiorum nostrum **obliviscamur**
I am afraid that we shall forget the courage of our
ancestors

paves ne ducas tu illam
You are afraid to marry her

Verres, **veritus ne** servi bellum in Sicilia **facerent**,
multos in vincula coniecit
Verres, fearing that slaves might revolt in Sicily, threw
many into prison

Romani **verebantur ne** fortiter **non pugnavissent**
The Romans were afraid that they had not fought
bravely

3   timeo **abire**
I am afraid to go away

mulier **timebat manere** sola
The woman was scared to remain alone

Conditional Sentences

Compare the following two sentences in English:

(a) If I tell you a lie, you will be angry
(b) If I were to tell you a lie, you would be angry

The first is a *logical statement of fact*, stating what *will* happen, the second is a *hypothesis*, stating what *would* happen.

For the first type of sentence, Latin uses the indicative mood in both main and conditional clauses. For the second type, Latin uses the subjunctive mood in both main and conditional clauses.

Translate type (a) as follows:

si hoc **dicis**, sapiens **es**
if you say this, you are wise

si hoc **dicebas**, sapiens **eras**
if you were saying this, you were wise

si hoc **dixisti**, erravisti
if you said this, then you made a mistake

si hoc **dixeris**, errabis
if you say this, you will make a mistake

Notice that the same tenses in English are used as in Latin except in the last sentence. Latin is more precise – you *will have said* this, before you make a mistake, therefore Latin uses the *future perfect* tense.

Continued

- Consider also the following sentence:

  si me **amabis**, mecum **manebis**
  If you love me, you will stay with me

  Latin uses the *future* tense in both clauses, English uses the *present* tense in the "if" clause. Both actions, "loving" and "remaining" *logically* refer to the *future*.

Translate type (b) as follows:

  (*present*)
  si hoc **dicas**, **erres**
  if you were to say this, you would be making a mistake

  (*imperfect*)
  si hoc **diceres**, **errares**
  if you said (*or* were saying) that, you would be making a mistake

  (*pluperfect*)
  si hoc **dixisses**, **erravisses**
  if you had said that, you would have made a mistake

Notice that both tenses of the subjunctive are the same in the above examples. Sometimes an imperfect may be used in one clause and the pluperfect in the other:

si pudorem **haberes**, Romā **abiisses**
if you had any sense of shame, you would have left Rome

Conditional Sentences (contd)

Negative Conditional Sentences

- **nisi** (unless) is the negative of **si** (if). (→**1**)
- **si non** (if not), is less common and negates *one* word, or is used when the same verb is repeated (→**2**)

1 **nisi** id statim **feceris**, ego te **tradam** magistratui
Unless you do this immediately, I shall hand you over
to the magistrate

nisi utilem **crederem**, non pacem **peterem**
Unless I thought it useful, I would not be seeking
peace

2 **si** me **adiuveris**, laeta **ero**; **si** me **non adiuveris**, tristis
ero
If you help me, I shall be happy; if you don't help me,
I shall be sad

si navigatio **non morabitur**, mox te **videbo**
If my sailing is not delayed, I shall see you soon

Further Examples

(**b**) quis illum sceleratum fuisse **putavisset**, **si tacuisset**?
Who would have thought he was a rascal, if he had
kept quiet?

(**b**) multi **agerent** et **pugnarent si** rei publicae **videretur**
Many would act and fight, if the state decided

(**a**) **gaudemus si** liberi in horto **ludunt**
We are happy if the children play in the garden

(**b**) **si quis** in caelum **ascendisset**, pulchritudinem side-
rum **conspexisset**
If anyone had gone up to heaven, he would have seen
the beauty of the stars

Concessive Clauses

In English, Concessive clauses usually begin with "although":

Although he is rich, he is not happy
I shall succeed although it is difficult

- **quamquam** (although) is followed by the indicative (→**1**)

  Note that **tamen** (however) is often used in the main clause in concessive sentences

- **quamvis** (although) is always followed by the subjunctive (→**2**)

- **cum** in the sense "although" is always followed by the subjunctive (→**3**)

- **etsi** (although) takes the indicative or subjunctive according to the same rules as **si** (*see p 106*). The indicative is more common (→**4**)

1 medici **quamquam intellegunt**, numquam **tamen**
aegris de morbo dicunt
Although doctors know, they never tell their patients
about their illness

quamquam Aeneas dicere **volebat**, Dido solo fixos
oculos aversa tenebat
Although Aeneas wished to speak, Dido turned away
and kept her eyes fixed on the ground

2 **quamvis** frater **esset** molestus, Marcus eum amavit
Although his brother was a nuisance, Marcus loved
him

feminae, **quamvis** in periculo **essent**, tamen liberos
servaverunt
Although the women were in danger, yet they saved
their children

3 **cum non didicissem** geometrias, litteras sciebam
Although I had not learnt geometry, I knew my letters

non poterant, **cum vellent**, Lucium liberare
They were not able, although they wished, to free
Lucius

4 **etsi** servus **est**, certe persona est
Although he is a slave, he is a person

etsi victoriam non **reportavissetis**, tamen vos con-
tentos esse oportebat
Although you had not won a victory, yet you should
have been content

etsi domi **esset filius iuvenis**, agros ipse colebat
Although he had a young son at home, he cultivated
the fields by himself

Causal Clauses

Clauses which begin with the words "because" or "since" and give a reason for something are often called causal clauses in English.

- Causal clauses have their verbs in the indicative when the *actual* cause is stated. They are introduced by **quod**, **quia** (because), and **quoniam** (since) (→**1**)

- **quod** is used with the subjunctive when the cause is only *suggested* (→**2**)

- **non quod** (+*subj*) ... **sed quia** (+*indic*) not because ... but because ..., is used when the first reason is discarded. The true reason is expressed in the indicative (→**3**)

- **cum** (since, as) is always followed by the subjunctive (→**4**)

- **qui** with the subjunctive can be used to mean "since" (→**5**)

1 non iratus sum **quod** in me **fuisti** asperior
I am not angry because you were too harsh towards me

in crypta Neapolitana vecti, timebamus **quia** longior et obscurior carcere **erat**
Travelling in the Naples tunnel, we were afraid because it was longer and darker than a prison

quoniam ita tu **vis**, ego Puteolos tecum proficiscar
Since you wish this, I shall set off with you to Pozzuoli

2 templa spoliare non poterant **quod** religione **impedirentur**
They could not plunder the temples because (they said) they were prevented by religious feelings

3 mater semper maxime laboravit **non quod** necessarium **esset sed quia** honestum esse **videbatur**
Mother always worked very hard, not because it was necessary but because it seemed proper

4 quae **cum** ita **sint**, Catilina, egredere ex urbe!
Since this is so, Catilina, leave the city!

Caesar, **cum** in continente hiemare **constitusset**, ad Galliam rediit
Since Caesar had decided to spend the winter on the mainland, he returned to Gaul

5 sapiens erat **qui** studiis totos annos **dedisset**
He was wise since he had devoted all his years to study

Temporal Clauses

Clauses denoting time are introduced by conjunctions, *eg*
ubi (when) followed by verbs in the indicative. Some
conjunctions, *eg* **cum** (when) may also take the subjunctive. (→**1**)

Conjunctions followed by the indicative:

ut	when, as
ubi	when
cum primum **ubi primum** **ut primum**	} as soon as
simul ac **simul atque**	} as soon as
quotiens	as often as, whenever
quamdiu	as long as, while
ex quo (tempore)	ever since
postquam **posteaquam**	} after (**post** or **postea** may be separated from **quam**)

Continued

1   **ut** valetudo Germanici Romae **nuntiata est**, magna ira
erat
When Germanicus' state of health was announced in
Rome, there was great anger

ubi primum classis visa est, **complentur** non modo
portus sed moenia ac tecta
As soon as the fleet was seen, not only the harbour
but the walls and rooftops were filled (with people)

quod **ubi cognitum est** hostibus, universi nonam legi-
onem nocte aggressi sunt
When this was discovered by the enemy, all of them
attacked the ninth legion at night

quotiens proficiscor, pluit
Every time I set out, it rains

manebat **quamdiu poterat**
He stayed as long as he could

septimus annus est, milites, **ex quo** Britanniam **vicistis**
It is seven years, soldiers, since you conquered Britain

postquam vallum **intravit**, portas stationibus **con-
firmavit**
After entering the fortification, he strengthened the
gates with guards

post tertium diem **quam redierat**, mortuus est
He died three days after his return

Temporal Clauses (contd)

Conjunctions which take the indicative or subjunctive:

cum

- **when** with indicative and often **tum** in the main clause (→**1**)

- **whenever** with the following pattern of tenses in the indicative: (→**2**)

  + **perfect** followed by **present** tense
  + **future perfect** followed by **future** tense
  + **pluperfect** followed by **imperfect** tense

- **when, as** with the imperfect or pluperfect subjunctive narrative (→**3**)

dum

- **while** with indicative

  the present tense is used when **dum** means "during the time that" (→**4**)

- Note that where the same tense (here, the future) is used in both clauses, **dum** means "all the time that". Latin uses future **vivam** more accurately than English "live" (→**5**)

Continued

1   **cum** tu Romae **eras**, **tum** ego domi eram
    When you were in Rome, I was then at home

2   **cum surrexerat**, **cadebat**
    Whenever he got up, he fell down

    cum domum **veni**, amicum **visito**
    Whenever I come home, I visit my friend

    Socrates, **cum** triginta tyranni **essent**, non exibat
    Socrates didn't go out when there were 30 tyrants

    cum id Caesari **nuntiatum esse** ab urbe profectus est
    When that message had been given to Caesar, he set
    out from the city

4   **dum** haec **geruntur** sex milia hominum ad Rhenum
    contenderunt
    While this was going on, 6000 men marched to the
    Rhine

5   **dum vivam**, laeta **ero**
    While I live, I shall be happy

Temporal Clauses (contd)

Clauses which take Indicative or Subjunctive (contd)

dum, donec

- **until** with subjunctive, often with the sense of purpose or suspense (→**1**)

antequam, priusquam

- **before** with indicative (→**2**)
- **ante** and **prius** may be separated from **quam** especially in negative sentences (→**3**)

- **before** with subjunctive, usually with a sense of purpose or limit (→**4**)

1 multa Antonio concessit **dum** interfectores patris **ulcisceretur**
He made many concessions to Antony until he could avenge his father's killers

Haterius in periculo erat **donec** Augustam auxilium **oraret**
Haterius was in danger until he begged for Augusta's help

2 **antequam finiam**, hoc dicam
Before I finish, I shall say this

priusquam gallus **cantabit**, ter me negabis
Before the cock crows, you will deny me three times

3 neque **prius** fugere destiterunt **quam** ad castra **pervenerunt**
They didn't stop running away before reaching their camp

4 consul Romam festinavit **antequam** Hannibal eo **perveniret**
The consul hurried to Rome before Hannibal could reach it

ita cassita nidum migravit **priusquam** agricola frumentum **meteret**
And so the lark abandoned her nest before the farmer could reap the corn

Comparative Clauses

- These are adverbial clauses which express likeness, agreement (or the opposite) with what is stated in the main clause. (→**1**)

- When the comparative clause states a fact (as above) the verb is in the **indicative**. The commonest words of comparison are (→**2**)

  ut (as), **sicut** (just as), **aliter ac**, **aliter ut** (different from), **idem ac**, **idem atque, qui** *etc* (the same as)

- When the comparative clause is purely **imaginary**, the verb is **subjunctive**. The commonest words used with this type of clause are (→**3**)

  velut(si), **quasi**, **tamquam (si)** (as if)

1   eadem dixi ac prius dixeram
      I said the same as I had said before

2   **ego ita ero, ut me esse oportet**
      I shall be as I should be

      sicut lupus agnos rapit, ita mater liberos servat
      Just as the wolf snatches the lamb, so the mother
      saves her children

      haud aliter se gerebat ac solebat
      He behaved as he usually did
  or He behaved no differently from usual

      idem abierunt qui venerant
      The same men vanished as came

3   **velutsi haec res nihil ad se pertinuisset, tacebat**
      He remained silent, as if this thing had nothing to
      do with him

      **hic flammae Aetnae minantur quasi ad caelum
      sublatae sint**
      Here Aetna's flames threaten, as if raised to the
      heavens

      Cleopatram salutaverunt **tamquam si esset** regina
      They greeted Cleopatra as if she were queen

Relative Clauses

- Relative clauses are more common in Latin than in English. They are introduced by the following:

qui, quae, quod	which, who, that
ubi	where, in which
unde	from where, from which

- These relatives come at the beginning of the clause but after prepositions.

- The relative agrees with a word which precedes it – its *antecedent* – in gender and number, but takes its case from its own clause (→**1**)

  qui is masculine plural agreeing with antecedent **Romani**, nominative because it is the subject of **incenderunt**

- **quā** is feminine singular agreeing with **regio**, ablative after preposition **in** (→**2**)

- **quos** is masculine plural agreeing with **servos**, accusative because it is the object of **iudicavit** (→**3**)

- The relative **quod** refers to a sentence, and **id** is omitted (**id quod** – that which). This is often used in parenthesis, and not attached grammatically to the rest of the sentence

  After **cuius** (of, concerning which) the noun **laudationis** is repeated (→**4**)

- The relative sometimes agrees with the following word, especially with the verb **esse** (→**5**)

Continued

1 hi sunt Romani **qui** libros incenderunt
These are the Romans who burnt the books

2 haec est regio **in qua** ego sum natus
This is the region in which I was born

3 servos **quos** ipse iudicavit, eos sua sponte liberavit
He willingly freed those slaves whom he himself had
judged

4 deinde, **quod** alio loco antea dixi, quae est ista tandem
laudatio, **cuius laudationis** legati et principes et publice
tibi navem aedificatam, et privatim se ipsos abs te
spoliatos esse dixerunt? (**Cicero**, Verres V 58)
Well then, as I said earlier elsewhere, what does that
praise consist of, namely that publicly the ambassadors
and chief citizens said a ship had been built for you,
but privately that they themselves had been robbed by
you?

5 iusta gloria **qui** fructus virtutis est, bello quaeritur
True glory, which is the reward of courage, is looked
for in war

Relative Clauses (contd)

Use Of Subjunctive In Relative Clauses

- The subjunctive is used in relative clauses dependent on infinitives or subjunctives (→**1**)

- When **qui** is used with the subjunctive, it may express cause (→**2**)

  quippe is sometimes used with **qui** in this sense

- When **qui** *etc* is used with the present or imperfect subjunctive, it may express purpose (→**3**)

- **qui** with the subjunctive is used with the following (→**4**)

dignus est **qui**	he is worthy of
idoneus est **qui**	he is fit to
sunt **qui**	there are people who
nemo est **qui**	there is no one who

- At the beginning of a sentence, any part of **qui**, **quae**, **quod** may be used as a connective (instead of the demonstrative) with the previous sentence. Translate it in English by "this" or "that" (→**5**)

1 quis sit **cui** vita talis **placeat**?
Who is there that likes such a life?

2 multa de mea sententia questus est Caesar (**quippe**)
qui Ravennae Crassum ante **vidisset**
Caesar complained a lot about my decision since he
had seen Crassus at Ravenna previously

3 legatos misit **qui** pacem **peterent**
He sent ambassadors to ask for peace

4 **Sunt qui** dicere **timeant**
There are some who are afraid to speak

nemo **idoneus** aderat **qui responderet**
There was nobody there capable of replying

5 **quod** cum **audivisset**, soror lacrimas fudit
When she heard this, my sister shed tears

quae cum ita **sint**, Vatinium defendam
Since this is so, I shall defend Vatinius

Negatives

There are several ways of forming a negative in Latin.

non

- This is the common negative in the indicative and usually stands before the verb, although it may be put in front of any word for emphasis (→**1**)

- Two negatives in the same sentence make an affirmative (→**2**)

haud

- This makes a single word negative, usually an adjective or an adverb (→**3**)

- It is also used in expressions such as **haud scio an** (I don't know whether), and **haud dubito** (I don't doubt) (→**4**)

- **haudquaquam** means not at all (→**5**)

Continued

1 ante horam tertiam noctis de foro **non discedit**
He didn't leave the forum before nine o'clock at night

Ambarri Caesarem certiorem faciunt se, vastatis agris,
non facile vim hostium ab oppidis prohibere
The Ambarri informed Caesar that it was **not easy** for
them, since their territory was destroyed, to keep the
enemy force away from their towns

Caesar **non exspectandum** sibi statuit dum Helvetii
pervenirent
Caesar decided **not to wait** till the Swiss arrived

2 **non** possum **non facere**
I must do

non sumus **ignari**
We are well aware

3 **haud** magnus
not great

haud procul
not far away

4 **haud scio an** ire mihi liceat
I don't know whether I am allowed to go

5 homo bonus, **haudquaquam** eloquens
A good man but not at all a good speaker

Negatives (contd)

ne

- This is the negative of the imperative and subjunctive. It is also used in many subordinate clauses where the verb is in the subjunctive (→**1**)
- Wishes (→**2**)
- Purpose (→**3**)
- Indirect command (→**4**)
- Fearing (→**5**)

Continued

1 **ne** diutius **vivemus**
Let us **not live** any longer

2 utinam **ne** id **accidisset**
I wish that it **had not happened**

3 agnus celeriter fugit **ne** lupi se **caperent**
The lamb ran away quickly **in case** the wolves caught
it

4 pater mihi imperavit **ne abirem**
Father told me **not to go away**

5 cives metuebant **ne** Tiberius libertatem sibi **non
redderet**
The citizens were afraid that Tiberius **would not give**
them **back** their freedom

veritus sum **ne** id quod accidit **adveniret**
I was afraid that what did in fact happen **might take
place**

Negatives (contd)

Other Negatives

- **neque ... neque**   neither ... nor (→**1**)
- **neque ... quisquam**   neither anyone *or* and no
                                one
  neque ... quidquam   neither anything *or* and
                                nothing
  neque ... umquam   neither ever *or* and never
  nemo ... umquam   no one ever *or* never
                                anyone
  nihil ... umquam   nothing ever *or* never
                                anything (→**2**)

- Notice the following combinations:

  nonnulli some   *but* **nulli ... non** all
  nonnihil somewhat *but* **nihil ... non** everything
                                                    (→**3**)

- **non solum ... sed etiam** ⎫ not only ... but also
  non solum ... sed quoque ⎭   (→**4**)

- Roman authors repeat negatives for effect (→**5**)

1 **neque** illo adit **quisquam neque** eis ipsis **quidquam**
praeter oram maritimam notum est
Neither did anyone approach that place, nor did they
themselves know anything except the coast

2 **neque** post id tempus **umquam** summis nobiscum
copiis hostes contenderunt
And after that the enemy never engaged in battle with
us at full strength

ego **nihil umquam** feci solus
I never did anything alone

3 **nonnulli** amici
some friends

nulli amici **non** venerunt
all my friends came

4 Herennius Pontius, iam gravis annis, **non solum** mi-
litaribus **sed quoque** civilibus muneribus abscesserat
Herennius Pontius, now old, had withdrawn not only
from military but also from civic duties

5 **nihil** audio quod audisse, **nihil** dico quod dixisse paeni-
teat; **nemo** apud me quemquam sinistris sermonibus
carpit, **neminem** ipse reprehendo, **nisi** tamen me cum
parum commode scribo; **nulla** spe, **nullo** timore sol-
licitor, **nullis** rumoribus inquietor; mecum tantum et
cum libellis loquor (**Pliny** Ep 1, 9)
I hear nothing that I would regret having heard, I say
nothing that I would regret having said; at home nobody nags me with vicious remarks, I don't blame
anyone except myself when I write badly; no hope or
fear worries me, no idle talk disturbs me; I speak only
to myself and to my books

Translation Guidelines

Translating from Latin into English can be both a challenge
and a pleasure. The word order of both languages is
different: word order shows the relationship of words in
English, in Latin it is shown by word endings. Sentences
are generally shorter in English, structures simpler. Latin
sentences often contain more subordinate clauses, sometimes embedded in other clauses, and often build up
to form a long periodic sentence. Subject matter is two
thousand years distant in time, although many ideas are
still familiar to us today. The following guidelines are
suggested to help in translation.

Guidelines

- *Establish the context* of the passage to be translated.
  Read the introduction in English carefully, find out
  who or *what* is being discussed, *when* and *where* the
  action took place.

- *Read through the whole passage* fairly quickly to gain
  some general understanding of the passage, however
  incomplete.

- *Focus on each sentence*, either taking each word as
  it comes, or establishing subject/verb/object according
  to your normal approach. Many find it helpful to pick
  out the verbs and work out the structure of the clauses.
  Watch for agreement of adjectives with nouns and how
  prepositional phrases fit in.

- *Watch conjunctions* **et**, **sed** *etc* and connectives such as **tamen** (however), and **igitur** (therefore). These help explain the logic of the passage as a whole.

- *Note punctuation*. It can be helpful in isolating clauses within the sentences, or marking off an ablative absolute.

- *Be open-minded*. Does **cum**, for example, mean "when", "since", or "although"? Don't decide till the whole sentence is worked out.

- *Use dictionaries carefully*. Check words of similar spelling, check endings. Once you have found the right Latin word, check all of its meanings before deciding on the correct translation.

- *Watch out for features of style eg* use of two adjectives with same meaning *etc*.

- Finally, *check your translation*. Does the narrative or logic of the passage seem consistent? Does your English sound natural? Does it represent the tone or style of the Latin passage? At this stage, fill in any blanks or make corrections.

Translation Problems

Finding the subject

- Look for a noun with a nominative ending. Check with verb ending for agreement. If there is no nominative, the subject will be indicated by the verb ending. Remember that, in Latin, the subject is continued from the previous sentence unless there is clear indication otherwise (→**1**)

Adjective agreement

- Check which adjective agrees with which noun in number, case and gender. Remember that it may be separated from its noun.

  <pre>   a   b b   a</pre>
  te **flagrantis atrox hora Caniculae** nescit tangere
  The blazing Dog Star's fierce daytime heat can't touch you

Passive

- Often it is better to turn a Latin passive verb into an active verb in English (→**2**)

Tense

- English is not so precise as Latin in its use of tenses. Use the tense that seems most natural in English, for example, English past tense for historic present in Latin, or English present tense for Latin future perfect in a conditional clause (→**3**)

Continued

1   **consules** et armare plebem et inermem pati
          timebant. **sedabant** tumultum, sedando interdum
          movebant.
          The consuls were afraid both to arm the people
          and to leave them unarmed. **They quelled** the riot,
          but sometimes, in quelling it, **they stirred it up
          again**.

2   hoc a tu **demonstrari** et **probari** volo
          I wish you to demonstrate and prove this
     or I wish this to be demonstrated and proved by you

3   hoc faciam si **potuero** (*future perfect*)
          I shall do this if I can (*present*)

Translation Problems (contd)

Ablative absolute

hostibus victis can be translated:

when the enemy had been beaten
after beating the enemy
they beat the enemy and ...
although the enemy were beaten

Choose the version that makes most sense within the context of the passage.

Omission of esse

- Parts of **esse** (to be) are often omitted and have to be supplied in English (→**1**)

Omission of small words (ut, id, eo, hic *etc*)

- Check that you do not omit to translate these words – they are often very important (→**2**)

Neuter plurals

- **omnia** (everything) and **multa** (many things) are often mistranslated.

Impersonal passives

- It is worthwhile learning these (→**3**)

Continued

1 sed Germanicus quanto (**erat**) summae spei propior,
    tanto impensius pro Tiberio niti
    But the nearer Germanicus **was** to succeeding, the
    more strenuously he exerted himself on behalf of
    Tiberius

2 **eo**   to there (*adv*), by, with *or* from
                     him (*abl of pronoun*)
    id … quod   that which
    hic   this (*pron*), here (*adv*)
    fit … ut   it happens … that

3 **allatum est**   it was announced
    cognitum est   it was discovered
    pugnatum est   a battle was fought
    traditum est   it was recorded
    visum est   it seemed

Translation Problems (contd)

Similarity of English/Latin Words

A higher percentage of English words are derived from Latin than from any other source. This can be helpful when trying to deduce the meaning of a Latin word, *eg* **portus** (port). But **porta** (gate) may cause confusion. The following examples taken from actual examination scripts provide a cautionary note. The correct translation follows in brackets:

prima luce nuntius hic **Ameriam** venit
At dawn the messenger came to America
(*At dawn the messenger came to Ameria*)

sex et quinquaginta **milia passuum** in cisio pervolavit
56 thousand flew past in a chariot
(*He quickly travelled fifty-six miles in a chariot*)

ut mori **mallet**
He would rather be killed by a mallet
(*To prefer to die*)

legati **crediderunt**
The embassy got credit
(*The ambassadors believed*)

False Friends/Confusables

ad (+ *acc*)	to, towards
ab (+ *abl*)	from, by, with
adeo	to such an extent
adeō	I approach
aestās	summer
aestus	heat, tide
aetas	age
aura	breeze
aurēs (*pl*)	ears
aurum	gold
avis	bird
avus	grandfather
cadō	I fall
caedō	I cut, kill
cēdō	I go, yield
campus	plain
castra (*pl*)	camp
cēterum	but
cēterī (*pl*)	the rest
coepī	I began
coēgi	I forced
constituō	I decide
consistō	I stop

Continued

crīmen	charge
scelus	crime
cum (*prep*)	with
cum (*conj*)	when, since, although
dominus	master
domus	house
equitēs (*pl*)	horsemen
equus	horse
fama	fame, report
fames	hunger
forte	by chance
fortis	brave (*not* strong)
fugāre	to put to flight
fugere	to flee, escape
hōra	hour
hōrum (*gen pl*)	of these
iaceō	I lie
iaciō	I throw
imperātor	general (*not* emperor)
imperātus	ordered (*past participle*)
inveniō	I find (*not* come in)
invītō	I invite
invītus	unwilling
iter, -ineris	journey
iterum	again
lātus, -a, -um	broad
lātus, -a, -um	brought
lătus, -eris	side

False Friends/Confusables (contd)

līber, -ri	book
līber, -a, -um	free
līberī, -orum (*pl*)	children
libertus, -i	freedman
magister, -ri	master
magistratus	magistrate
malus, -a, -um	bad
mālum, -i	apple
mālo, mālle	I prefer
manus, -ūs	hand, band
mānēs, -ium	spirits of dead
miser, -a, -um	unhappy
mīseram	I had sent (*plup of* **mitto**)
morior, -ī	I die
moror, -ārī	I delay
nauta	sailor
nāvis	ship
nēmō	no one
nimium	too much
occāsio	opportunity
occāsus (solis)	setting (of sun)
occidere	to fall, set
occīdere	to kill
opem	help
opera, -ae	work
opus, -eris	task
opus est	it is necessary

Continued

ōra, -ae	coast
orō, -āre	I pray, beg
ōs, ōris	face
ŏs, ŏssis	bone
parcō, -ere	I spare
pareō, -ēre	I obey
pario, -ere	I give birth to
parō, -āre	I prepare
passus, -us	a pace
passus, -a, -um	suffered (*past participle of* **patior**)
porta, -ae	gate
portus, -us	port
portō, -āre	I carry
quaerō, -ere	I seek
queror, -ī	I complain
quīdam	a certain (person)
quĭdem	indeed
reddō, -ere	I give back
redeō, -īre	I go back
serviō, -īre	I serve
servō, -āre	I save
sōl, -is	sun
soleō, -ēre solitus sum	I am accustomed
solum, -i	soil
sōlus, -a, -um	alone

False Friends/Confusables (contd)

tamen	however
tandem	at last
ut(ī)	in order that, as, when
utī (*dep*)	to use
vallis, -is	valley
vallum, -i	wall, rampart
victor	winner
victus (*past part*)	beaten
vinctus (*past part*)	bound
vīs	force
vīres, -ium	strength
vir, -ī	man
virga, -ae	stick
virgō, -inis	girl
vīta, -ae	life
vītō, -āre	I avoid

VERB TABLES

Conjugations

There are four patterns of regular Latin verbs called conjugations. Each can be identified by the ending of the
present infinitive:

- First conjugation verbs end in -**āre** (*eg* am**āre** – to
  love)
- Second conjugation verbs end in -**ēre** (*eg* hab**ēre** – to
  have)
- Third conjugation verbs end in -**ere** (*eg* mitt**ere** – to
  send)
- Fourth conjugation verbs end in -**īre** (*eg* aud**īre** – to
  hear)

Each regular verb has three **stems**:

- A **present stem** which is found by cutting off -re from the present infinitive (*eg* am**ā**re, hab**ē**re, mit**t**ere, aud**ī**re).

- A **perfect stem** which is formed by adding **-v** to the present stem in the first and fourth conjugations (*eg* amav**ī**, audiv**ī**), and by adding **-u** to the present stem in the second conjugation (*eg* habu**ī**).

  In the third conjugation there are several possible endings (*eg* scr**ī**ps**ī**, d**ī**x**ī**).

  Some short verbs lengthen the stem vowel (*eg* l**ē**g**ī**), others double the first consonant and vowel (*eg* cu-curri).

- A **supine stem** which is formed by cutting off **-um** from the supine forms (*eg* am**ā**tum, hab**i**tum, mis**s**um, aud**ī**tum).

Tenses

These forms of the verb show when an action takes place, in the present, in the past or in the future.

In Latin there are six tenses:

1	Present	
2	Imperfect	} formed from the **present** stem
3	Future	
4	Perfect	
5	Pluperfect	} formed from the **perfect** stem
6	Future Perfect	

Tenses Formed from the Present Stem

The following endings are added to the stem:

	PRESENT Conj 1&2	IMPERFECT	FUTURE	Conj 3&4
sing				
1st person	-ō	-bam	-bō	-am
2nd person	-s	-bas	-bis	-ēs
3rd person	-t	-bat	-bit	-et
pl				
1st person	-mus	-bāmus	-bimus	-ēmus
2nd person	-tis	-bātis	-bitis	-ētis
3rd person	-nt	-bant	-bunt	-ent

Note that the above endings show the number and person of the subject of the verb. Subject pronouns are therefore not normally necessary in Latin.

Continued

Conjugations

1	2	3	4

INFINITIVE

amāre	habēre	mittere	audīre

PRESENT STEM

amā-	habē-	mitte-	audī-

PRESENT

amō	habeō	mittō	audiō
amās	habēs	mittis	audīs
amat	habet	mittit	audit
amā**mus**	habē**mus**	mitti**mus**	audī**mus**
amā**tis**	habē**tis**	mitti**tis**	audī**tis**
ama**nt**	habe**nt**	mittu**nt**	audiu**nt**

IMPERFECT

amā**bam**	habē**bam**	mittē**bam**	audiē**bam**
amā**bās**	habē**bās**	mittē**bās**	audiē**bās**
amā**bat**	habē**bat**	mittē**bat**	audiē**bat**
amā**bāmus**	habē**bāmus**	mittē**bāmus**	audiē**bamus**
amā**bātis**	habē**bātis**	mittē**bātis**	audiē**bātis**
amā**bant**	habē**bant**	mittē**bant**	audiē**bant**

FUTURE

amā**bō**	habē**bō**	mitt**am**	audi**am**
amā**bis**	habē**bis**	mitt**ēs**	audi**ēs**
amā**bit**	habē**bit**	mitt**et**	audi**et**
amā**bimus**	habē**bimus**	mitt**ēmus**	audi**ēmus**
amā**bitis**	habē**bitis**	mitt**ētis**	audi**ētis**
amā**bunt**	habē**bunt**	mitt**ent**	audi**ent**

Tenses (contd)

Use:

The Present

In Latin, the present tense expresses what is going on now and can be translated into English in two ways (*eg* **laborat** – he works, he is working)

- The present is often used in Latin instead of a past tense to make the action more exciting (→**1**)

- Sometimes the Latin present tense is used to describe an action begun in the past and and still continuing (→**2**)

The Imperfect

- Describes what went on or continued for a time (→**3**)

- Denotes an action repeated in the past (→**4**)

- Is used when an action is intended or interrupted (→**5**)

- Is sometimes translated "had" when used with **iam** (→**6**)

The Future

- Is used in Latin as in English to denote what will or is going to be or to happen (→**7**)

- Is occasionally used as a command (→**8**)

- After "**si**" (if) in conditional sentences, it is sometimes translated as present tense in English (→**9**)

1　**prima luce Caesar Gallos oppugnat**
　　Caesar attacked the Gauls at dawn

2　**Alexander iam tres annos regit**
　　Alexander has been ruling for three years now

3　**pluebat** – it was raining

4　**fortiter pugnabant**
　　They used to fight bravely
　or They kept fighting bravely

5　**Romam intrabam**
　　I was about to enter Rome

6　**multos iam dies villam habitabat**
　　He had already lived in the house for many days

7　**hoc faciemus**
　　We shall do this
　or We are going to do this

　　erit gloria
　　There will be glory

8　**non me vocabis**
　　Don't call me

9　**si id credes, errabis**
　　If you believe this, you will be making a mistake

Tenses (contd)

Tenses Formed from the Perfect Stem

To the appropriate perfect stem add the following endings:

sing	PERFECT	PLUPERFECT	FUTURE PERFECT
1st person	-ī	-eram	-erō
2nd person	-istī	-erās	-eris
3rd person	-it	-erat	-erit

pl			
1st person	-imus	-erāmus	-erimus
2nd person	-istis	-erātis	-eritis
3rd person	-ērunt	-erant	-erint

Continued

Conjugations

1	**2**	**3**	**4**
PERFECT STEM			
amāv-	habu-	mīs-	audī-
PERFECT			
amāvī	habuī	mīsī	audīvi
amāvistī	habuistī	mīsistī	audīvistī
amāvit	habuit	mīsit	audīvit
amāvimus	habuimus	mīsimus	audīvimus
amāvistis	habuistis	mīsistis	audīvistis
amāvērunt	habuērunt	mīsērunt	audīvērunt
PLUPERFECT			
amāveram	habueram	mīseram	audīveram
amāverās	habuerās	mīserās	audīverās
amāverat	habuerat	mīserat	audīverat
amāverāmus	habuerāmus	mīserāmus	audīverāmus
amāverātis	habuerātis	mīserātis	audīverātis
amāverant	habuerant	mīserant	audīverant
FUTURE PERFECT			
amāverō	habuerō	mīserō	audīverō
amāveris	habueris	mīseris	audīveris
amāverit	habuerit	mīserit	audīverit
amāverimus	habuerimus	mīserimus	audīverimus
amāveritis	habueritis	mīseritis	audīveritis
amāverint	habuerint	mīserint	audīverint

Tenses (contd)

Use:

The Perfect

- In Latin, the perfect tense is equivalent to the simple past tense (*eg* **vīdī** – I saw) and the perfect tense (*eg* **vīdī** – I have seen) in English.

- It states past action particularly in narrative (→**1**)

- Expresses an action completed in the past which still has effect in the present (→**2**)

The Pluperfect

- Denotes an action completed in the past before another past action (→**3**)

The Future Perfect

- Denotes completing something in the future (→**4**)

- Is often used with **volō**, **possum**, **nolō** *etc* (→**5**)

- Denotes an action which precedes another action in the future, often in a subordinate clause (→**6**)

1 veni, vidi, vici
I came, I saw, I conquered

2 spem in fide alicuius habuerunt
They place their hope in someone's good faith

3 Mithridates urbem Asiae clarissimam obsederat quam L. Lucullus virtute liberavit
Mithridates had besieged the most famous city in Asia that Lucius Lucullus freed by his courage

4 id fecero
I shall have done it

5 si potuero, faciam
If I can, I shall do it

6 qui prior venerit, prior discedet
First to come will be first to go

The Passive

Verbs may be active or passive. In **active** forms of the verb, the subject carries out the action (*eg* Brutus **killed** Caesar). In **passive** forms of the verb, the subject receives the action (*eg* Caesar **was killed** by Brutus).

Conjugation

To form the passive tenses of regular verbs, substitute the following endings for those of the present, imperfect and future active tenses (conjugated on page 148):

- In the present 1st person sing the ending is -**or**.
- In the imperfect, the endings are added to -**ba**.
- In the future (conjugations 1 and 2), the endings are added to -**bo** (*1st person sing*), -**be** (*2nd person sing*), and -**bi** for other persons. In conjugations 3 and 4, the 1st person *sing* ending is -**ar**.

Continued

sing	1st person	-r
	2nd person	-ris
	3rd person	-tur
pl	1st person	-mur
	2nd person	-minī
	3rd person	-ntur

Conjugations

1	2	3	4

PRESENT PASSIVE

1	2	3	4
am**or**	habē**or**	mitt**or**	audi**or**
am**āris**	habē**ris**	mitt**eris**	aud**īris**
am**ātur**	habē**tur**	mitt**itur**	aud**ītur**
am**āmur**	habē**mur**	mitt**imur**	aud**īmur**
am**āminī**	habē**minī**	mitt**iminī**	aud**īminī**
am**antur**	habē**ntur**	mitt**untur**	audi**untur**

IMPERFECT PASSIVE

1	2	3	4
am**ābar**	habē**bar**	mitt**ēbar**	audi**ēbar**
am**ābāris**	habē**bāris**	mitt**ēbāris**	audi**ēbāris**
am**ābātur**	habē**bātur**	mitt**ēbātur**	audi**ēbātur**
am**ābāmur**	habē**bāmur**	mitt**ēbāmur**	audi**ēbāmur**
am**ābāminī**	habē**bāminī**	mitt**ēbāminī**	audi**ēbāminī**
am**ābantur**	habē**bantur**	mitt**ēbantur**	audi**ēbantur**

FUTURE PASSIVE

1	2	3	4
am**ābor**	habē**bor**	mitt**ar**	audi**ar**
am**āberis**	habē**beris**	mitt**ēris**	audi**ēris**
am**ābitur**	habē**bitur**	mitt**ētur**	audi**ētur**
am**ābimur**	habē**bimur**	mitt**ēmur**	audi**ēmur**
am**ābiminī**	habē**biminī**	mitt**ēminī**	audi**ēminī**
am**ābuntur**	habē**buntur**	mitt**entur**	audi**entur**

The Passive (contd)

Translation

Present Passive

1. I am loved   we are loved
   you (*sing*) are loved   you (*pl*) are loved
   he/she/it is loved   they are loved

2. I am held *etc*

3. I am sent *etc*

4. I am heard *etc*

Imperfect Passive

1. I was loved   we were loved
   you (*sing*) were loved   you (*pl*) were loved
   he/she/it was loved   they were loved

2. I was held *etc*

3. I was sent *etc*

4. I was heard *etc*

Future Passive

1. I shall be loved   we shall be loved
   you (*sing*) will be loved   you (*pl*) will be loved
   he/she/it will be loved   they will be loved

2. I shall be held *etc*

3. I shall be sent *etc*

4. I shall be heard *etc*

● "going to be" may also be used to translate the future.
Continued

The Passive (contd)

Perfect, Pluperfect and Future Perfect Passive

These tenses consist of the past participle (formed from the supine stem) and tenses of the verb **sum** (to be). The past participle endings agree in number and gender with the subject of the verb.

Conjugations

1	2	3	4	
PERFECT PASSIVE				
amātus	habitus	missus	audītus	**sum**
-a, -um	-a, -um	-a, -um	-a, -um	**es**
				est
amātī	habitī	missī	audītī	**sumus**
-ae, -a	-ae, -a	-ae, -a	-ae, -a	**estis**
				sunt
PLUPERFECT PASSIVE				
amātus	habitus	missus	audītus	**eram**
				erās
				erat
amātī	habitī	missī	audītī	**erāmus**
				erātis
				erant
FUTURE PERFECT PASSIVE				
amātus	habitus	missus	audītus	**erō**
				eris
				erit
amātī	habitī	missī	audītī	**erimus**
				eritis
				erunt

The Passive (contd)

Translation

Perfect Passive

1 I have been loved   we have been loved
   you (*sing*) have been   you (*pl*) have been loved
    loved   they have been loved
   he/she/it has been loved
2   I have been held *or* I was held *etc*
3   I have been sent *or* I was sent *etc*
4   I have been heard *or* I was heard *etc*

Pluperfect Passive

1 I had been loved   we had been loved
   you (*sing*) had been loved   you (*pl*) had been loved
   he/she/it had been loved   they had been loved
2   I had been held *etc*
3   I had been sent *etc*
4   I had been heard *etc*

Future Perfect Passive

1 I shall have been loved   we shall have been loved
   you (*sing*) will have been   you (*pl*) will have been
    loved   loved
   he/she/it will have been   they will have been loved
    loved
2   I shall have been held *etc*
3   I shall have been sent *etc*
4   I shall have been heard *etc*

1 **milites a populo occisi sunt**
   The soldiers were killed by the people

2 **populus milites occidit**
   The people killed the soldiers

● Note that the subject of the passive verb in (1) becomes
  the object of the active verb in (2).

● Often in English it is better to translate the meaning
  actively as in (2).

● The **agent** of the action is translated by **a(b)** with the
  ablative case as in **a populo** (1) – by the people.

● The **thing** causing the action is translated by the ablative case alone

   saxo percussus erat
   He had been struck by a rock

The Subjunctive

So far all verbs described have belonged to the indicative mood, which states facts. The subjunctive mood represents ideas, possibilities or necessities and is often translated by auxiliary verbs such as **may**, **might**, **could**, **would**, **should** or **must**. There are four tenses active and passive – present, imperfect, perfect and pluperfect.

Formation of Active

The present subjunctive active is formed from the present stem, the imperfect from the infinitive. To these add the endings

-m, -s, -t, -mus, -tis, -nt.

● Note that in first conjugation present the preceding vowel is **-e**, and in all others **-a**.

● The present subjunctive active is sometimes translated by using "**may**" (→**1**)

● The imperfect subjunctive active is sometimes translated by using "**might**" (→**2**)

Continued

Conjugations

1	**2**	**3**	**4**

PRESENT SUBJUNCTIVE ACTIVE

amem	habeam	mittam	audiam
amēs	habeās	mittās	audiās
amet	habeat	mittat	audiat
amēmus	habeāmus	mittāmus	audiāmus
amētis	habeātis	mittātis	audiātis
ament	habeant	mittant	audiant

IMPERFECT SUBJUNCTIVE ACTIVE

amārem	habērem	mitterem	audīrem
amārēs	habērēs	mitterēs	audīrēs
amāret	habēret	mitteret	audīret
amārēmus	habērēmus	mitterēmus	audīrēmus
amārētis	habērētis	mitterētis	audīrētis
amārent	habērent	mitterent	audīrent

1 **amem** – I may love
mittas – you (*sing*) may send
habeat – he may have
audiant – they may hear

2 **mitteretis** – you (*pl*) might send
haberem – I might have
amaret – she might love
audirent – they might hear

The Subjunctive (contd)

Formation of Passive

The passive of the present and imperfect subjunctive is easily formed by substituting the normal passive endings (**-r**, **-ris**, **-tur**, **-mur**, **-mini**, **-ntur**) for the active ones.

Conjugation

1	2	3	4
PRESENT SUBJUNCTIVE PASSIVE			
amer	habear	mittar	audiar
amēris	habeāris	mittāris	audiāris
amētur	habeātur	mittātur	audiātur
amēmur	habeāmur	mittāmur	audiāmur
amēminī	habeāminī	mittāminī	audiāminī
amentur	habeantur	mittantur	audiantur
IMPERFECT SUBJUNCTIVE PASSIVE			
amārer	habērer	mitterer	audīrer
amārēris	habērēris	mitterēris	audīrēris
amārētur	habērētur	mitterētur	audīrētur
amārēmur	habērēmur	mitterēmur	audīrēmur
amārēminī	habērēminī	mitterēminī	audīrēminī
amārentur	habērentur	mitterentur	audīrentur

- The present subjunctive passive is sometimes translated by using "**may be**" (→**1**)
- The imperfect subjunctive passive is sometimes translated by using "**might be**" (→**2**)

Continued

1 **habeamur** – we may be held
   amer – I may be loved
   mittamini – you (*pl*) may be sent
   audiantur – they may be heard

2 **audiremini** – you (*pl*) might be heard
   amaretur – he might be loved
   haberentur – they might be held
   mitterer – I might be sent

The Subjunctive (contd)

Perfect and Pluperfect Subjunctive Active

Both perfect and pluperfect subjunctive active are formed from the perfect stem as follows:

Conjugation

1	2	3	4
PERFECT SUBJUNCTIVE ACTIVE			
amā**verim**	habu**erim**	mīs**erim**	audī**verim**
amā**veris**	habu**eris**	mīs**eris**	audī**veris**
amā**verit**	habu**erit**	mīs**erit**	audī**verit**
amā**verimus**	habu**erimus**	mīs**erimus**	audī**verimus**
amā**veritis**	habu**eritis**	mīs**eritis**	audī**veritis**
amā**verint**	habu**erint**	mīs**erint**	audī**verint**
PLUPERFECT SUBJUNCTIVE ACTIVE			
amā**vissem**	habu**issem**	mīs**issem**	audī**vissem**
amā**vissēs**	habu**issēs**	mīs**issēs**	audī**vissēs**
amā**visset**	habu**isset**	mīs**isset**	audī**visset**
amā**vissēmus**	habu**issēmus**	mīs**issēmus**	audī**vissēmus**
amā**vissētis**	habu**issētis**	mīs**issētis**	audī**vissētis**
amā**vissent**	habu**issent**	mīs**issent**	audī**vissent**

- The Perfect subjunctive active is sometimes translated by using "**may have**" with the past participle in English (→**1**)

- The Pluperfect subjunctive active is sometimes translated by using "**might have**" with the past participle in English (→**2**)

Continued

1   **miserit** – he may have sent
    habuerint – they may have had
    audiveris – you (*sing*) may have heard
    amaveritis – you (*pl*) may have loved

2   **amavissemus** – we might have loved
    habuisset – he might have had
    audivissent – they might have heard
    misissem – I might have sent

The Subjunctive (contd)

Perfect and Pluperfect Subjunctive Passive

Both perfect and pluperfect subjunctive passive are formed from the supine stem and the present and imperfect subjunctive of **sum** respectively:

Conjugation

	1		**2**
PERFECT SUBJUNCTIVE PASSIVE			
amātus	**sim**	habitus	**sim**
	sīs		**sīs**
	sit		**sit**
pl			
amātī	**sīmus**	habitī	**sīmus**
	sītis		**sītis**
	sint		**sint**

	1		**2**
PLUPERFECT SUBJUNCTIVE PASSIVE			
amātus	**essem**	habitus	**essem**
	essēs		**essēs**
	esset		**esset**
pl			
amātī	**essēmus**	habitī	**essēmus**
	essētis		**essētis**
	essent		**essent**

Continued

Conjugation

	3		**4**

PERFECT SUBJUNCTIVE PASSIVE

missus	**sim**	audītus	**sim**
	sīs		**sīs**
	sit		**sit**

pl

missī	**sīmus**	audītī	**sīmus**
	sītis		**sītis**
	sint		**sint**

PLUPERFECT SUBJUNCTIVE PASSIVE

missus	**essem**	auditus	**essem**
	essēs		**essēs**
	esset		**esset**

pl

missī	**essēmus**	audītī	**essēmus**
	essētis		**essētis**
	essent		**essent**

The Subjunctive (contd)

- The perfect subjunctive passive is sometimes translated by using "**may have been**" with the past participle in English (→**1**)

- The pluperfect subjunctive passive is sometimes translated by using "**might have been**" with the past participle in English (→**2**)

1 **habitus sis** – you (*sing*) may have been held
   missi simus – we may have been sent
   auditus sim – I may have been heard
   amati sint – they may have been loved

2 **amati essemus** – we might have been loved
   habiti essent – they might have been held
   missus esses – you (*sing*) might have been sent
   auditus essem – I might have been heard

The Imperative

This is the mood of command. It has two forms, 2nd person *sing* and *pl*, active (→**1**) and passive: (→**2**)

Conjugations

	1	**2**	**3**	**4**
IMPERATIVE ACTIVE				
sing	am**ā**	hab**ē**	mitt**e**	aud**ī**
pl	am**āte**	hab**ēte**	mitt**ite**	aud**īte**
IMPERATIVE PASSIVE				
sing	am**āre**	hab**ēre**	mitt**ere**	aud**īre**
pl	am**āmini**	hab**ēmini**	mitt**īmini**	aud**īminī**

1 **pecuniam mittite, o cives**
Citizens, send money! (active)

   spem habe
Have hope! (active)

2 **in curia audimini**
Be heard in the senate! (passive)

   ab omnibus semper amare, Romule
Always be loved by everyone, Romulus (passive)

The Infinitive

The infinitive was originally a noun and can be used in this way in Latin (*eg* **amāre** – to love *or* loving). There are three types, present, future and perfect, both active and passive, formed as follows:

Active

	1	**2**
PRESENT	amā**re**	habē**re**
FUTURE	amāt**ūrus esse**	habit**ūrus esse**
PERFECT	amāv**isse**	habu**isse**

	3	**4**
PRESENT	mitte**re**	audī**re**
FUTURE	miss**ūrus esse**	audīt**ūrus esse**
PERFECT	mīs**isse**	audīv**isse**

Translation

to love	to have
to be going to love	to be going to have
to have loved	to have had
to send	to hear
to be going to send	to be going to hear
to have sent	to have heard

Continued

Passive

	1	**2**
PRESENT	am**ārī**	hab**ērī**
FUTURE	amāt**um īrī**	habit**um īrī**
PERFECT	amāt**us esse**	habit**us esse**

	3	**4**
PRESENT	mitt**ī**	aud**īrī**
FUTURE	miss**um īrī**	audīt**um īrī**
PERFECT	miss**us esse**	audīt**us esse**

Translation

to be loved	to be had
to be going to be loved	to be going to be had
to have been loved	to have been had
to be sent	to be heard
to be going to be sent	to be going to be heard
to have been sent	to have been heard

- In the future active -**urus**, -**a**, -**um** and in the perfect passive -**us**, -**a**, -**um** agree in number and gender with the noun or pronoun in indirect speech.

The Infinitive (contd)

Uses of the Infinitive

- It can be used as a neuter noun
- As the subject of the sentence (→**1**)
- With certain nouns such as **fas** (right), **nefas** (wrong) (→**2**)
- As the object of the following verbs: (→**3**)

volō	I wish	**cupiō**	I desire
nolō	I do not wish	**sinō**	I allow
possum	I am able to, can	**cogō**	I force
sciō	I know (how)	**audeō**	I dare
nesciō	I do not know	**conor**	I try
debeō	I ought	**desinō**	I stop
soleō	I am accustomed	**dubitō**	I hesitate
incipiō	I begin	**coepi**	I begin

- It can be used to describe a rapid series of events instead of using the perfect tense (→**4**)

1 errare est humanum
To err is human

2 nefas est templa destruere
It is wrong to destroy temples

3 volo domum redire
I wish to return home

desine mortuos commemorare
Stop remembering the dead

Romam exstinctam esse cupit
He wishes Rome blotted out

4 ille non tollere oculos, non remittere stilum, tum fragor adventare et intra limen audiri
He did not raise his eyes nor put down his pen, then the noise came closer and could be heard inside the door.

Participles

There are three participles (or verbal adjectives) in Latin:
the present active, the perfect passive and the future active.

The Present Participle

This is formed from the present stem by adding **-ns** and
lengthening the previous vowel. The genitive ending is
-ntis.

Conjugation

1	**2**	**3**	**4**
am**āns**	hab**ēns**	mitt**ēns**	audi**ēns**
loving	having	sending	hearing

- Note that these decline like group 3 adjectives ending
  in **-ns** with ablative singular, in **-i** when used as an
  adjective and in **-e** when used as a verb. They agree in
  number, case and gender with nouns or pronouns in
  the sentence.

Use

- It denotes an action going on at the same time as the
  main verb (→**1**)
- It can be used as a noun (→**2**)

Continued

1   **pro patria pugnantes iuvenes mortui sunt**
          The young men died *while fighting* for their country

          Romulo regnante, Roma urbs parva erat
          While Romulus was ruling, Rome was a small city

2   **lacrimae adstantium**
          the tears of *people standing by*

Participles (contd)

The Perfect Participle

This is formed from the supine stem by adding the endings
-**us**, -**a**, -**m**. It declines like first and second declension
adjectives (*see pages 25–28*)

Conjugation

1	2	3	4
amāt**us**	habit**us**	miss**us**	audīt**us**
(having been) loved	(having been) held	(having been) sent	(having been) heard

Use

- It denotes an action that is completed before that of
  the main verb (→**1**)
- English is less precise in the use of tenses and frequently
  uses a present to translate a Latin past participle.

The Future Participle

This is formed by adding -**urus**, -**a**, -**um** to the supine stem.
It declines like first and second declension adjectives.

Conjugation

1	2	3	4
amāt**ūrus**	habit**ūrus**	miss**ūrus**	audīt**ūrus**
going to love	going to have	going to send	going to hear

Use

- It denotes an action that is going to take place (→**2**)
- The forms **futurus** (going to be) and **venturus** (going
  to come) are often used as adjectives.

1   **equites Romani auditi ad senatum adducti sunt**
The Roman businessmen *were heard* and then were
brought before the Senate

castra capta incendimus
We *captured* the camp and burnt it
or Capturing the camp, we burnt it

2   **nos morituri te salutamus**
We who are about to die salute you

Gerunds and Gerundives

The **gerund** is a **verbal noun** and is active.

The **gerundive** is a **verbal adjective** and is passive.

The gerund is formed by adding -**ndum** to the present stem. It declines like a neuter noun -**ndum**, -**ndī**, -**ndō**, -**ndō**.

The gerundive declines like first and second declension adjectives -**us**, -**a**, -**um** (A)

Conjugation

1	**2**	**3**	**4**

GERUND

ama**ndum**	habe**ndum**	mitte**ndum**	audie**ndum**
loving	having	sending	hearing

GERUNDIVE

ama**ndus**	habe**ndus**	mitte**ndus**	audie**ndus**
requiring to be loved	requiring to be held	requiring to be sent	requiring to be heard

Gerunds and Gerundives (contd)

Use of Gerund and Gerundive

- The gerund is often used with the accusative case to express **purpose** (→**1**)

- If the verb has a direct object, the gerundive is used instead (→**2**)

- The gerund is used in the genitive case with nouns and adjectives (→**3**) such as

  ars (art), **spes** (hope), **cupidus** (eager), **peritus** (skilled)

- Both the gerund and the gerundive can be used in the genitive with **causa** to express **purpose** (→**4**)

- The gerundive can be used to imply **obligation** and the person is expressed by the dative case (→**5**)

- If the verb cannot take a direct object, the impersonal form is used (→**6**)

- Both the gerund and the gerundive can be used in the ablative case (→**7**)

1   **venit ad regnandum**
He came to rule

2   **venit ad pacem petendam**
He came to make peace

3   **spes videndi**
Hope of seeing

      peritus equitandi
Skilled in riding

4   **dicendi causa**
to speak

      pacis petendae causa
For the sake of making peace

5   **poenae nobis timendae sunt**
Punishment must be feared by us
or We must fear punishment

6   **mihi parendum est**
You must obey me

7   **docendo discimus**
We learn by teaching

      me puniendo effugit
By punishing me he escaped

Impersonal Verbs

Impersonal verbs are used in the third person singular only

- To describe the weather (→**1**)

- To express feeling. The person affected appears in the accusative case and the cause in the genitive case (→**2**)

- To express permission or pleasure. The person affected appears in the accusative in the dative case. The verb is often followed by a present infinitive (→**3**)

- To express happening, following *etc*. These are followed by **ut** with the subjunctive mood (→**4**)

fit ut	it happens that
accidit ut	it happens that
sequitur ut	it follows that

- Certain intransitive verbs are used impersonally in the passive (→**5**)

- Verbs of saying, believing *etc* are used impersonally in the perfect passive tense (→**6**)

- The verbs, **interest** (it is of importance), and **refert** (it is of concern), are followed usually by **meā**, **tuā**, **nostrā**, **vestrā** (→**7**)

- Sometimes **interest** is followed by genitive of the person (→**8**)

- The following verbs are followed by a present infinitive. The person involved appears in the accusative case (→**9**)

me decet	it is fitting for me
me oportet	I must/ought

1 **pluit**
it is raining

tonat
there is thunder

fulgurat
there is lightning

ningit
it is snowing

2 **me miseret**
I am sorry for

me paenitet
I repent of

me pudet
I am ashamed of

me taedet
I am tired of

me miseret sociorum
I am sorry for my
comrades

3 **mihi licet**
I am allowed to

tibi videtur
it seems good to you
or you decide

nobis placet
it is pleasing to us
or we like

vobis placuit
discedere
you (*pl*) decided to
leave

4 **fit ut**
it happens that

accidit ut
it happens that

sequitur ut
it follows that

fit ut fallar
it happens that I am
mistaken

5 **pugnatum est in mari**
the battle was fought at sea

vivitur in oculis omnium
life is lived in the sight of everyone

6 **nuntiatum est**
it has been announced

creditum est
it has been believed

mihi dictum est Germanos transiisse Rhenum
I was told that the Germans had crossed the Rhine

Deponent Verbs

Deponent verbs are passive in form but active in meaning. They also have present and future participles and future infinitive which are active. The perfect participle is also active in meaning. Otherwise the conjugation is similar to that of regular verbs.

1st Conjugation

conārī (to try)

INDICATIVE		SUBJUNCTIVE	
PRESENT			
conor	I try *etc*	coner	I may try *etc*
conāris		conēris	
conātur		conētur	
conāmur		conēmur	
conāminī		conēmini	
conantur		conentur	
IMPERFECT			
conābar	I was trying	conārer	I might try *etc*
conābāris	*etc*	conārēris	
conābātur		conārētur	
conābāmur		conārēmur	
conābāmini		conārēmini	
conabantur		conārentur	
FUTURE			
conābor	I shall try *etc*		
conāberis			
conābitur			
conābimur			
conābimini			
conābuntur			

Continued

PERFECT

| conātus | **sum** | I tried | conātus | **sim** | I may have tried |
| -a, -um | **es** | you tried *etc* | -a, -um | **sis** | you may have tried *etc* |

PLUPERFECT

| conātus | **eram** | I had tried | conātus | **essem** | I might have tried |
| -a, -um | **eras** | you had tried *etc* | -a, -um | **esses** | you might have tried *etc* |

FUTURE PERFECT

| conātus | **ero** | I shall have tried |
| -a, -um | **eris** | you will have tried *etc* |

IMPERATIVE

| conāre | *sing* | try |
| conāminī | *pl* | try |

INFINITIVES

present	conārī	to try
future	conātūrus esse	to be going to try
perfect	conātus esse	to have tried

PARTICIPLES

present	conāns	trying
future	conātūrus	going to try
perfect	conātus	having tried

| *GERUND* | conāndum | trying |

| *GERUNDIVE* | conāndus | requiring to be tried |

Second, Third, Fourth Conjugations

These are conjugated like the passive form of verbs of the corresponding conjugations. A summary is provided as follows:

Second Conjugation

verēri (to fear, be afraid)

INDICATIVE

Present	verē**or**	I am afraid
Imperfect	verēba**r**	I was afraid
Future	verēbo**r**	I shall be afraid
Perfect	verit**us sum**	I was afraid
Pluperfect	verit**us eram**	I had been afraid
Future Perfect	verit**us erō**	I shall have been afraid

SUBJUNCTIVE

Present	verē**ar**	I may be afraid
Imperfect	verē**rer**	I might be afraid
Perfect	verit**us sim**	I may have been afraid
Pluperfect	verit**us essem**	I might have been afraid

IMPERATIVE

Singular	verē**re**	be afraid
Plural	verē**minī**	be afraid

Continued

INFINITIVES

Present	ver**ērī**	to be afraid
Future	verit**ūrus esse**	to be going to be afraid
Perfect	verit**us esse**	to have been afraid

PARTICIPLES

Present	ver**ēns**	fearing, being afraid
Future	verit**ūrus**	going to fear *or* be afraid
Perfect	verit**us**	having feared *or* been afraid (active)

GERUND	ver**endum**	fearing
GERUNDIVE	ver**endus**	requiring to be feared

Second, Third, Fourth Conjugations
(contd)

Third Conjugation

sequī (to follow)

INDICATIVE

Present	sequ**or**	I follow
Imperfect	sequ**ēbar**	I was following
Future	sequ**ar**	I shall follow
Perfect	secūt**us sum**	I followed
Pluperfect	secūt**us eram**	I had followed
Future Perfect	secūt**us erō**	I shall have followed

SUBJUNCTIVE

Present	sequ**ar**	I may follow
Imperfect	sequ**erer**	I might follow
Perfect	secūt**us sim**	I may have followed
Pluperfect	secūt**us essem**	I might have followed

IMPERATIVE

Singular	sequ**ere**	follow
Plural	sequ**iminī**	follow

INFINITIVES

Present	sequ**ī**	to follow
Future	secūt**ūrus esse**	to be going to follow
Perfect	secūt**us esse**	to have followed

PARTICIPLES

Present	sequ**ēns**	following
Future	secūt**ūrus**	going to follow
Perfect	secūt**us**	having followed
GERUND	seque**ndum**	following
GERUNDIVE	seque**ndus**	requiring to be followed

Fourth Conjugation

mentīrī (to lie)

INDICATIVE

Present	ment**ior**	I lie
Imperfect	mentiē**bar**	I was lying
Future	menti**ar**	I shall lie
Perfect	mentī**tus sum**	I lied
Pluperfect	mentī**tus eram**	I had lied
Future Perfect	mentī**tus erō**	I shall have lied

SUBJUNCTIVE

Present	menti**ar**	I may lie
Imperfect	mentī**rer**	I might lie
Perfect	mentī**tus sim**	I may have lied
Pluperfect	mentī**tus essem**	I might have lied

IMPERATIVE

Singular	ment**ire**	lie
Plural	ment**iminī**	lie

INFINITIVES

Present	ment**irī**	to lie
Future	mentit**ūrus esse**	to be going to lie
Perfect	mentī**tus esse**	to have lied

PARTICIPLES

Present	mentiē**ns**	lying
Future	mentī**turus**	going to lie
Perfect	mentī**tus**	having lied

GERUND	mentie**ndum**	lying
GERUNDIVE	mentie**ndus**	requiring to be lied to

Semi-deponent Verbs

A few verbs are passive in form and active in meaning in only the perfect tenses. All other tenses are active in form and meaning. These are:

audēre	to dare
gaudēre	to be glad
solēre	to be accustomed
confidere	to trust

INDICATIVE

Present	aude**ō**	I dare
Imperfect	audē**bam**	I was daring
Future	audē**bo**	I shall dare

SUBJUNCTIVE

Present	aude**am**	I may dare
Imperfect	audē**rem**	I might dare

IMPERATIVE

Singular	aud**ē**	dare
Plural	audē**tē**	dare

INFINITIVE

Present	audē**re**	to dare

PRES PARTICIPLE	audē**ns**	daring
GERUND	aude**ndum**	daring
GERUNDIVE	aude**ndus**	requiring to be dared

All other parts are **passive** in form:

INDICATIVE

Perfect	aus**us sum**	I dared
Pluperfect	aus**us eram**	I had dared
Future Perfect	aus**us erō**	I shall have dared

SUBJUNCTIVE

Perfect	aus**us sim**	I may have dared
Pluperfect	aus**us essem**	I might have dared

PARTICIPLES

Perfect	aus**us**	having dared
Future	aus**ūrus**	going to dare

INFINITIVES

Perfect	aus**us esse**	to have dared
Future	aus**ūrus esse**	to be going to dare

Unique Verbs

The following verbs are different from the conjugations described so far:

esse (to be)

Indicative

PRESENT

sum	I am
es	you (*sing*) are
est	he/she/it is
sumus	we are
estis	you (*pl*) are
sunt	they are

IMPERFECT

eram	I was
erās	you (*sing*) were
erat	he/she/it was
erāmus	we were
erātis	you (*pl*) were
erant	they were

FUTURE

erō	I shall be
eris	you (*sing*) will be
erit	he/she/it will be
erimus	we shall be
eritis	you (*pl*) will be
erunt	they will be

Subjunctive

PRESENT

sim	I may be
sīs	you (*sing*) may be
sit	he/she/it may be
sīmus	we may be
sītīs	you (*pl*) may be
sint	they may be

IMPERFECT

essem	I might be
essēs	you (*sing*) might be
esset	he/she/it might be
essēmus	we might be
essētis	you (*pl*) might be
essent	they might be

Continued

esse (to be) (contd)

Indicative

PERFECT

fuī	I have been, was
fuistī	you (*sing*) have been/were
fuit	he/she/it has been/was
fuimus	we have been/were
fuistis	you (*pl*) have been/were
fuērunt	they have been/were

PLUPERFECT

fueram	I had been
fuerās	you (*sing*) had been
fuerat	he/she/it had been
fuerāmus	we had been
fuerātis	you (*pl*) had been
fuerant	they had been

FUTURE PERFECT

fuerō	I shall have been
fuerīs	you (*sing*) will have been
fuerit	he/she/it will have been
fuerīmus	we shall have been
fuerītis	you (*pl*) will have been
fuerint	they will have been

Subjunctive

PERFECT
fuerim	I may have been
fuerīs	you (*sing*) may have been
fuerit	he/she/it may have been
fuerīmus	we may have been
fuerītis	you (*pl*) may have been
fuerint	they may have been

PLUPERFECT
fuissem	I might have been
fuissēs	you (*sing*) might have been
fuisset	he/she/it might have been
fuissēmus	we might have been
fuissētis	you (*pl*) might have been
fuissent	they might have been

Imperative
Singular	**es**	be
Plural	**este**	be

Infinitives
Present	**esse**	to be
Future	**futūrus esse**	to be going to be
Perfect	{ **fore** **fuisse**	to have been

Participle
	futūrus	going to be

- Compounds of **esse** are listed in the principal parts page 220.

posse (to be able)

● This verb is formed from **pot-** and **-esse**. Note that **t** becomes **s** before another **s**.

Indicative

PRESENT

possum	I am able
potes	you (*sing*) are able
potest	he/she/it is able
possumus	we are able
potestis	you (*pl*) are able
possunt	they are able

IMPERFECT

poteram	I was able *etc*
poterās	
poterat	
poterāmus	
poterātis	
poterant	

FUTURE

poterō	I shall be able *etc*
poteris	
poterit	
poterimus	
poteritis	
poterunt	

Subjunctive

PRESENT
possim   I may be able *etc*
possis
possit
possīmus
possītīs
possint

IMPERFECT
possem   I might be able *etc*
possēs
posset
possēmus
possētis
possent

Continued

posse (to be able) (contd)

Indicative

PERFECT
potuī   I have been able *etc*
potuistī
potuit
potuimus
potuistis
potuērunt

PLUPERFECT
potueram   I had been able *etc*
potuerās
potuerat
potuerāmus
potuerātis
potuerant

FUTURE PERFECT
potuerō   I shall have been able *etc*
potueris
potuerit
potuerimus
potueritis
potuerint

Subjunctive

PERFECT
potuerim   I may have been able *etc*
potueris
potuerit
potuerimus
potueritis
potuerint

PLUPERFECT
potuissem   I might have been able *etc*
potuissēs
potuisset
potuissēmus
potuissētis
potuissent

Infinitives
posse   to be able
potuisse   to have been able

ferre (to bear)

Active
Indicative

PRESENT
ferō   I bear *etc*
fers
fert
ferimus
fertis
ferunt

IMPERFECT
ferēbam   I was bearing

FUTURE
feram   I shall bear

PERFECT
tuli   I bore

PLUPERFECT
tuleram   I had borne

FUTURE PERFECT
tulerō   I shall have borne

Subjunctive

PRESENT
feram I may bear *etc*
ferās
ferat
ferāmus
ferātis
ferant

IMPERFECT
ferrem I might bear

PERFECT
tulerim I may have borne

PLUPERFECT
tulissem I might have borne

Infinitives
Present **ferre** to bear
Future **lātūrus esse** to be going to bear
Perfect **tulisse** to have borne

Imperatives
Singular **fer** bear
Plural **ferte** bear

Supine **lātum**

Continued

ferre (to bear) (contd)

Passive

Indicative

PRESENT
feror   I am borne *etc*
ferris
fertur
ferimur
feriminī
feruntur

IMPERFECT
ferēbar   I was being borne

FUTURE
ferar   I shall be borne

PERFECT
lātus sum   I was borne

PLUPERFECT
lātus eram   I had been borne

FUTURE PERFECT
lātus erō   I shall have been borne

Subjunctive

PRESENT
ferar   I may be borne *etc*
ferāris
ferātur
ferāmur
ferāminī
ferantur

IMPERFECT
ferrer   I might be borne

PERFECT
lātus sim   I may have been borne

PLUPERFECT
lātus essem   I might have been borne

Infinitives
Present   **ferri**   to be borne
Future   **lātum īrī**   to be going to be borne
Perfect   **lātus esse**   to have been borne

Imperatives
Singular   **ferre**   be borne
Plural   **feriminī**   be borne

Participles
Present   **ferēns**   bearing
Future   **lātūrus**   going to bear
Perfect   **lātus**   having been borne/carried

Gerund   **ferendum**   bearing

Gerundive   **ferendus**   requiring to be borne

Continued

fieri (to become, be made)

● This verb is the passive form of **facere** – to make.

Indicative

PRESENT
fīō   I become
fīs   you (*sing*) become
fit   he/she/it becomes
(fimus)
(fitis)
funt

IMPERFECT
fiēbam   I was becoming

FUTURE
fīam   I shall become

PERFECT
factus sum   I became

PLUPERFECT
factus eram   I had become

FUTURE PERFECT
factus erō   I shall have become

Subjunctive

PRESENT
fīam I may become *etc*
fīās
fīat
fīāmus
fīātis
fīant

IMPERFECT
fierem I might become

PERFECT
factus sim I may have become

PLUPERFECT
factus essem I might have become

Infinitives

Present	**fierī**	to become
Future	**factum īrī**	to be going to become
Perfect	**factus esse**	to have become

Participle

| Perfect | **factus** | having become |

Gerundive faciendus becoming

īre (to go)

- The stem is i-. Before a, o, u, it changes to e-.

Indicative

PRESENT
eo   I go *etc*
īs
it
īmus
ītis
eunt

IMPERFECT
ībam   I was going

FUTURE
ībō   I shall go

PERFECT
īvī or **iī**   I went/have gone

PLUPERFECT
īveram   I had gone

FUTURE PERFECT
īverō   I shall have gone

Subjunctive

PRESENT
eam   I may go *etc*
eās
eat
eāmus
eātis
eant

IMPERFECT
īrem   I might go

PERFECT
īverim   I may have gone

PLUPERFECT
īvissem   I might have gone

Infinitives

Present	**īre**	to go
Future	**ītūrus esse**	to be going to go
Perfect	**īvisse** *or* **īsse**	to have gone

Imperative

Singular	**ī**	go
Plural	**īte**	go

Participles

Present	**iēns** (*gen* **euntis**)	going
Future	**itūrus**	going to go

Gerund

eundum	going

velle (to wish)

Indicative

PRESENT
volō   I wish/am willing *etc*
vīs
vult
volumus
vultis
volunt

IMPERFECT
volēbam   I was wishing
volēbās
volēbat
volēbāmus
volēbātis
volēbant

FUTURE
volam   I shall wish

PERFECT
voluī   I wished/have wished

PLUPERFECT
volueram   I had wished

FUTURE PERFECT
voluerō   I shall have wished

Subjunctive

PRESENT
velim   I may wish
velīs
velit
velīmus
velītis
velint

IMPERFECT
vellem   I might wish
vellēs
vellet
vellēmus
vellētis
vellent

PERFECT
voluerim   I may have wished

PLUPERFECT
voluissem   I might have wished

Infinitives
Present	**velle**	to wish
Perfect	**voluisse**	to have wished

Participle   **volēns, -entis**   wishing

Continued

nōlle (not to wish, to be unwilling)

● This verb was originally **nōn volo**.

Indicative

PRESENT
nolō   I do not wish *etc*
nōn vīs
nōn vult
nōlumus
nōn vultis
nōlunt

IMPERFECT
nōlēbam   I was not wishing
nōlēbās
nōlēbat
nōlēbāmus
nōlēbātis
nōlēbant

FUTURE
nōlam   I shall not wish

PERFECT
nōlui   I have not wished

PLUPERFECT
nōlueram   I had not wished

FUTURE PERFECT
nōluerō   I shall not have wished

Continued

Subjunctive

PRESENT
nōlim   I may not wish
nōlīs
nōlit
nōlīmus
nōlītis
nōlint

IMPERFECT
nōllem   I might not wish
nōllēs
nōllet
nōllēmus
nōllētis
nōllent

PERFECT
nōluerim   I may not have wished

PLUPERFECT
nōluissem I might not have wished

Infinitives
Present   **nōlle**   not to wish
Perfect   **nōluisse**   not to have wished

Participle   **nōlēns, -entis**   not wishing

mālle (to prefer)

● This verb is formed from **ma volō** or **magis volō** (I wish more).

Indicative

PRESENT
mālō   I prefer
māvīs
māvult
mālumus
māvultis
mālunt

IMPERFECT
mālēbam   I was preferring
mālēbās
mālēbat
malebamus
mālēbātis
mālēbant

FUTURE
mālam   I shall prefer

PERFECT
mālui   I preferred

PLUPERFECT
mālueram   I had preferred

FUTURE PERFECT
māluerō   I shall have preferred

Subjunctive

PRESENT
mālim   I may prefer
mālīs
mālit
mālīmus
mālītis
mālint

IMPERFECT
māllem   I might prefer
māllēs
māllet
māllēmus
māllētis
māllent

PERFECT
māluerim   I may have preferred

PLUPERFECT
māluissem   I might have preferred

Infinitives
Present   **mālle**   to prefer
Perfect   **māluisse**   to have preferred

Defective Verbs

The following verbs have only a few forms which are used.
These are shown below.

inquam (I say)

PRESENT
inquam
inquis
inquit
īnquimus
inquitis
inquiunt

This verb is mainly used in the third person singular

inquiēbat	he said
inquiet	he will say
inquit	he said

avēre	to hail, say "hello"
salvēre	to hail
valēre	to say goodbye

● These verbs are found mainly in infinitives as above
  or imperatives:

avē, salvē	hello (*sing*)
avēte, salvēte	hello (*pl*)
valē (*sing*), **valēte** (*pl*)	goodbye

- Four verbs, **ōdī**, **meminī**, **coepī**, **nōvī** are found only in the perfect stem but are translated as follows:

ōdī	I hate
ōderam	I hated
ōderō	I shall hate
odisse	to hate
meminī	I remember
memineram	I remembered
meminerō	I shall remember
meminisse	to remember
coepī	I begin
coeperam	I began
coeperō	I shall begin
coepisse	to begin
nōvī	I know
nōveram	I knew
nōvero	I shall know
nōvisse	to know

Likewise subjunctive:

ōderim	I may hate
ōdissem	I might hate
meminerim	I may remember
meminissem	I might remember
coeperim	I may begin
coepissem	I might begin
nōverim	I may know
nōvissem	I might know

Principal Parts of Common Verbs

Latin verbs are most usefully listed under four principal parts, from which all other tenses *etc* may be formed or recognized

	1ST PERSON PRESENT ACTIVE	PRESENT INFINITIVE	1ST PERSON PERFECT ACTIVE	SUPINE
1st Conjugation	amō	amāre	amāvī	amātum
2nd Conjugation	habeō	habēre	habuī	habitum
3rd Conjugation	mittō	mittere	mīsī	missum
4th Conjugation	audiō	audīre	audīvī	auditum

400 of the most common verbs in Latin are listed below. Included are the following:

- 120 regular verbs. Their conjugations are indicated by numbers 1–4. All parts of these verbs can be deduced from the model conjugations on pp 148–185.

- Nearly 300 verbs which are irregular in parts (highlighted in bold), mainly in the perfect and supine. Again their conjugation is indicated by the number of the group to which they belong. Regular parts of these verbs and person endings etc may be deduced from the models of conjugations 1–4. Many compound verbs are included (*eg* afficio from ad-facio).

- Eight unique verbs and their compounds. These are marked bold throughout and a page reference is given *in italics* for these.

- Defective verbs which are shown in full in the main text. Again a page reference *in italics* is provided.

		Conj *Page*
abdō, abdere, **abdidī**, **abditum**	hide	3
abeō, abīre, abiī, abitum	go away	
abicio, abicere, **abiēcī**, **abiectum**	throw away	3
absum, abesse, afuī	be away	
accēdō, accēdere, **accessī**, **accessum**	approach	3
accidō, accidere, **accidī**	happen	3
accipiō, accipere, **accēpī**, **acceptum**	receive	3
accūsō, accūsāre, accūsāvī, accūsātum	accuse	1
addō, addere, **addidī**, **additum**	add	3
adeō, adīre, adiī, aditum	approach	
adimō, adimere, **adēmī**, **ademptum**	take away	3
adiuvō, adiuvare, **adiūvī**, **adiūtum**	help	1
administrō, administrāre, administrāvī, administratum	administer	1
adsum, adesse, adfuī	be present	
adveniō, advenīre, **advēnī**, **adventum**	reach	4
aedificō, aedificāre, aedificāvī, aedificātum	build	1
afferō, afferre, attulī, allātum	bring to	
afficiō, afficere, **affēcī**, **affectum**	affect	3
aggredior, aggredī, **aggressus sum**	attack	3
agnōscō, agnōscere, **agnōvī**, **agnitum**	recognize	3
agō, agere, **ēgī**, **āctum**	do/drive	3
alō, alere, **aluī**, **altum**	feed	3
ambulō, ambulāre, ambulāvī, ambulātum	walk	1
āmittō, āmittere, **āmīsī**, **āmissum**	lose	3
amō, amāre, amāvī, amātum	love	1

		Conj *Page*
animadvertō, animadvertere, **animadvertī, animadversum**	notice	**3**
aperiō, aperīre, **aperuī, apertum**	open	**4**
appareō, apparēre, appāruī, apparitum	appear	2
appellō, appellāre, appellāvī, appellātum	call	1
appropinquō, appropinquāre, appropinquāvī, appropinquātum	approach	1
arbitror, arbitrārī, arbitrātus sum	think	1
arcessō, arcessere, **arcessīvī, arcessītum**	send for	**3**
ārdeō, ārdēre, **ārsī, ārsum**	burn	**2**
armō, armāre, armāvī, armātum	arm	1
ascendō, ascendere, **ascendī, ascēnsum**	climb up	**3**
aspiciō, aspicere, **aspexī, aspectum**	look at	**3**
attingō, attingere, **attigī, attactum**	touch	**3**
audeō, audēre, **ausus sum**	dare	**2**
audiō, audīre, audīvī, audītum	hear	4
auferō, auferre, abstulī, ablātum	take away	
augeō, augēre, **auxī, auctum**	increase	**2**
bibō, bibere, **bibī**	drink	**3**
cadō, cadere, **cecidī, cāsum**	fall	**3**
caedō, caedere, **cecīdī, caesum**	cut/kill	**3**
canō, canere, **cecinī, cantum**	sing	**3**
capiō, capere, **cēpī, captum**	take	**3**
careō, carēre	lack	2
carpō, carpere, **carpsī, carptum**	pick	**3**
caveō, cavēre, **cāvī, cautum**	beware	**2**
cedō, cedere, **cessī, cessum**	go/give way	**3**

		Conj *Page*
cēlō, cēlāre, cēlāvī, cēlātum	hide	1
cernō, cernere, **crēvī, crētum**	perceive	3
cieō, ciēre, **cīvī, citum**	rouse	2
cingō, cingere, **cinxī, cinctum**	surround	3
circumdō, circumdāre, **circumdēdī, circumdātum**	place round	1
clāmo, clamāre, clamāvī, clamātum	shout	1
claudō, claudere, **clausī, clausum**	close	3
coepī, coeptus	begin	*219*
cōgitō, cōgitāre, cōgitāvī, cōgitātum	think	1
cōgnōscō, cōgnōscere, **cōgnōvī, cōgnitum**	find out	3
cogō, cōgere, **coēgī, coāctum**	collect/compel	3
colō, colere, **coluī, cultum**	look after/ worship	3
collocō, collocāre, collocāvī, collocātum	place	1
commoveō, commovēre, **commōvī, commōtum**	upset	2
comparō, comparāre, comparāvī, comparātum	get ready	1
comperiō, comperīre, **comperī, compertum**	discover	4
compleō, complēre, **complēvī, complētum**	fill	2
comprehendō, comprehendere, **comprehendī, comprehēnsum**	grasp	3
concurrō, concurrere, **concurrī, concursum**	run together	3
condō, condere, **condidī, conditum**	found	3
conficiō, conficere, **confēcī, confectum**	finish	3
confido, confīdere, **confīsus sum**	trust	3

		Conj *Page*
confīrmō, confīrmāre, confīrmāvī, confīrmātum	strengthen	1
confiteor, confitērī, **confēssus sum**	confess	**2**
congredior, congredī, **congressus sum**	meet	**3**
coniciō, conicere, **coniēci, coniectum**	throw	**3**
coniungō, coniungere, **coniūnxi, coniūnctum**	join	**3**
coniūro, coniūrāre, coniūrāvī, coniūrātum	conspire	1
conor, conārī, conātus sum	try	1
consentiō, consentire, **consēnsī, consēnsum**	agree	**4**
consistō, consistere, **constitī, constitum**	stop	**3**
conspiciō, conspicere, **conspexī, conspectum**	catch sight of	**3**
constō, constāre, **constitī**	agree	**1**
constituō, constituere, **constituī, constitūtum**	decide	**3**
construō, construere, **constrūxī, constructum**	construct	**3**
consulo, consulere, **consului, consultum**	consult	**3**
consūmō, consūmere, **consūmpsī, consūmptum**	use up	**3**
contemnō, contemnere, **contempsī, contemptum**	despise	**3**
contendō, contendere, **contendī, contentum**	strive/hurry	**3**
contingō, contingere, **contigī, contactum**	touch	**3**

		Conj *Page*
convenīo, convenīre, **convēni**, **conventum**	meet	**4**
corripio, corripere, **corripuī**, **correptum**	seize	**3**
crēdo, crēdere, **crēdidī**, **crēditum**	believe	**3**
crescō, crescere, **crēvī**, **crētum**	grow	**3**
culpō, culpāre, culpāvī, culpātum	blame	1
cunctor, cunctārī, cunctātus sum	delay	1
cupiō, cupere, **cupīvī**, **cupītum**	desire	**3**
cūrō, cūrāre, cūrāvī, curātum	look after	1
currō, currere, **cucurrī**, **cursum**	run	**3**
custōdio, custōdīre, custōdīvī, custōdītum	guard	**4**
damnō, damnāre, damnāvī, damnātum	condemn	1
dēbeō, dēbēre, dēbuī, dēbitum	have to/owe	2
dēdō, dēdere, **dēdidī**, **dēditum**	hand over/ yield	**3**
dēdūcō, dēdūcere, **dēdūxī**, **dēdūctum**	bring/escort	**3**
dēfendō, dēfendere, **dēfendi**, **dēfensum**	defend	**3**
dēficiō, dēficere, **dēfecī**, **dēfectum**	revolt/fail	**3**
dēiciō, dēicere, **dēiecī**, **dēiectum**	throw down	**3**
dēlectō, dēlectāre, dēlectāvī, dēlectatum	delight	1
dēleō, dēlere, **dēlēvī**, **dēlētum**	destroy	**2**
dēligō, dēligere, **dēlēgī**, **dēlectum**	choose	**3**
dēmōnstrō, dēmōnstrāre, dēmōnstrāvī, dēmōnstrātum	show	1
dēpōnō, dēpōnere, **dēposuī**, **dēpositum**	lay down	**3**

		Conj *Page*
dēscendō, dēscendere, **dēscendī**, **dēscensum**	go down	3
dēsero, dēsere, **dēseruī**, **dēsertum**	desert	3
dēsiderō, dēsiderāre, dēsiderāvī, dēsiderātum	long for	1
dēsiliō, dēsilere, **dēsiluī**, **dēsultum**	jump down	3
dēsino, dēsinere, **desiī**, **dēsitum**	stop/leave off	3
dēsistō, dēsistere, **dēstitī**	stop/leave off	3
dēspērō, dēspērāre, dēspērāvī, dēsperātum	despair	1
dēstruō, dēstruere, **dēstruxī**, **dēstructum**	destroy	3
dīcō, dīcere, **dīxī**, **dictum**	tell/say	3
dīligō, dīligere, **dīlexī**, **dīlēctum**	love	3
dīmittō, dīmittere, **dīmīsī**, **dīmissum**	send away	3
discēdō, discēdere, **discessī**, **discessum**	go away	3
discō, discere, **didicī**	learn	3
dīvidō, dīvidere, **dīvīsī**, **dīvīsum**	divide	3
dō, dāre, **dedī**, **datum**	give	1
doceō, docēre, docuī, **doctum**	teach	2
doleō, dolēre, doluī, dolitum	grieve	2
dormiō, dormīre, dormīvī, dormītum	sleep	4
dubitō, dubitāre, dubitāvī, dubitātum	doubt	1
dūcō, dūcere, **dūxī**, **ductum**	lead	3
ēdō, ēdere, **ēdī**, **ēsum**	eat	3
efficiō, efficere, **effēcī**, **effectum**	complete	3
effugiō, effugere, **effūgī**	escape	3
ēgredior, ēgredī, **egressus sum**	go out	3
ēmō, ēmere, **ēmī**, **ēmptum**	buy	3
eō, **īre**, **īvī**, **itum**	go	210

		Conj *Page*
errō, errāre, errāvī, errātum	wander/be wrong	1
ērumpō, ērumpere, **ērūpī**, **ēruptum**	burst out	**3**
excitō, excitāre, excitāvī, excitātum	arouse	1
exeō, exīre, exiī, exitum	go out	
exerceō, exercēre, exercuī, exercitum	exercise/train	2
exīstimō, exīstimāre, exīstimāvī, exīstimātum	think	1
expellō, expellere, **expulī**, **expulsum**	drive out	**3**
experior, experīrī, **expertus sum**	try/test	**4**
exspectō, exspectāre, exspectāvī, exspectātum	wait for	1
exuō, exuere, **exuī**, **exūtum**	take off	**3**
faciō, facere, **fēcī**, **factum**	do/make	**3**
fallō, fallere, **fefellī**, **falsum**	deceive	**3**
faveō, favēre, **fāvī**, **fautum**	favour	2
ferō, ferre, tulī, lātum	bring/bear	*204*
festīnō, festīnāre, festīnāvi, festīnātum	hurry	1
fīgo, fīgere, **fīxī**, **fīxum**	fix	**3**
fingō, fingere, **finxī**, **fictum**	invent	**3**
fīō, fierī, factus sum	become/ happen	*208*
flectō, flectere, **flexī**, **flexum**	bend	**3**
fleō, flēre, **flēvī**, **flētum**	weep	2
fluō, fluere, **flūxī**, **flūxum**	flow	**3**
frangō, frangere, **frēgī**, **frāctum**	break	**3**
fruor, fruī, **frūctus** *or* **fruitus sum**	enjoy	**3**
fugiō, fugere, **fūgī**, **fugitum**	flee/escape	**3**
fugō, fugāre, fugāvī, fugātum	put to flight	1
fundō, fundere, **fūdī**, **fūsum**	pour	**3**
fungor, fungi, **fūnctus sum**	perform	**3**

		Conj *Page*
gaudeō, gaudēre, **gāvīsus sum**	be glad	2
gemō, gemere, **gemuī, gemitum**	groan	3
gerō, gerere, **gessī, gestum**	carry on/ wear	3
gignō, gignere, **genuī, genitum**	produce	3
habeō, habēre, habuī, habitum	have/keep	2
habitō, habitāre, habitāvī, habitātum	live (in)	1
haereō, haerēre, **haesī, haesum**	stick	2
hauriō, haurīre, **hausī, haustum**	drain away	4
horreō, horrēre, horruī	stand on end	2
hortor, hortārī, hortātus sum	encourage	1
iaceō, iacēre, iacui	lie down	2
iaciō, iacere, **iēcī, iactum**	throw	3
ignōscō, īgnōscere, **īgnōvī, ignōtum**	forgive	3
immineō, imminēre	threaten	2
impediō, impedīre, impedīvī, impedītum	hinder	4
impellō, impellere, **impulī, impulsum**	drive on	3
imperō, imperāre, imperāvī, imperātum	order	1
incendō, incendere, **incendī, incēnsum**	burn	3
incipiō, incipere, **coepī, coeptum**	begin	3
incitō, incitāre, incitāvī, incitātum	drive on	1
inclūdō, inclūdere, **inclūsī, inclūsum**	include	3
incolō, incolere, **incoluī**	live (in)	3
īnferō, inferre, intulī, illātum	bring against	
ingredior, ingredī, **ingressus sum**	enter	3

		Conj *Page*
īnstituō, īnstituere, **īnstituī**, **īnstitūtum**	set up	**3**
īnstruō, īnstruere, **īnstrūxī**, **īnstrūctum**	set/draw up	**3**
intellegō, intellegere, **intellēxī**, **intellēctum**	realize	**3**
interficiō, interficere, **interfēcī**, **interfectum**	kill	**3**
intersum, interesse	be among/be important	(impers)
intrō, intrāre, intrāvī, intrātum	enter	1
inveniō, invenīre, **invēnī**, **inventum**	come upon/ find	**4**
invitō, invītāre, invītāvī, invītātum	invite	1
irrumpō, irrumpere, **irrūpī**, **irruptum**	rush into	**3**
iubeo, iubēre, **iussī**, **iussum**	order	**2**
iūdicō, iūdicāre, iūdicāvī, iūdicātum	judge	1
iungō, iungere, **iūnxī**, **iūnctum**	join	**3**
iūrō, iūrāre, iūrāvī, iūrātum	swear	1
iuvō, iuvāre, **iūvī**, **iūtum**	help	**1**
lābor, lābī, **lāpsus sum**	slip	**3**
labōrō, labōrāre, labōravī, labōrātum	work	1
lacessō, lacessere, **lacessīvī**, **lacessītum**	harass	**3**
lacrimō, lacrimāre, lacrimāvī, lacrimātum	weep	1
laedō, laedere, **laesī**, **laesum**	hurt	**3**
lateō, latēre, latuī	lie hidden	**2**
laudō, laudāre, laudāvī, laedātum	praise	1
lavō, lavāre, **lāvī**, **lautum**/lavātum/ **lōtum**	wash	**1**
legō, legere, **lēgī**, **lēctum**	read/choose	**3**

		Conj *Page*
levō, levāre, levāvī, levātum	lighten	1
līberō, līberāre, līberāvi, līberātum	free	1
licet, licēre, licuit	it is allowed	**2**
locō, locāre, locāvī, locātum	place	1
loquor, loquī, **locūtus sum**	speak	**3**
lūdō, lūdere, **lūsī**, **lūsum**	play	**3**
lustrō, lustrāre, lustrāvī, lustrātum	purify/scan	1
mālo, mālle, māluī	prefer	*216*
mandō, mandāre, mandāvī, mandātum	command/trust	1
maneō, manēre, **mānsī**, **mānsum**	remain/stay	**2**
meminī, meminisse	remember	*219*
mentior, mentīrī, mentītus sum	tell lies	4
metūō, metuere, **metuī**	fear	**3**
minor, minārī, minātus sum	threaten	1
minuō, minuere, **minuī**, **minūtum**	lessen	3
miror, mirārī, mirātus sum	wonder (at)	1
misceō, miscēre, **miscui**, **mixtum**	mix	**2**
{ misereor, miserērī, miseritus sum	pity	2
miseret, miserēre, miseruit		
(*eg* me miseret tui – I am sorry for you)		
mittō, mittere, **mīsī**, **missum**	send	**3**
mōlior, mōlīrī, mōlītūs sum	strive/toil	**4**
moneō, monēre, monuī, monitum	advise/warn	2
morior, morī, **mortuus sum**	die	**3**
moror, morāri, morātus sum	delay/loiter	1
moveō, movēre, **mōvī**, **mōtum**	move	**2**
mūniō, mūnīre, mūnīvī/mūniī, mūnītum	fortify	4
mūtō, mūtāre, mūtāvī, mūtātum	change	1
nancīscor, nancīscī, **na(n)ctus sum**	obtain	**3**
nārrō, nārrāre, nārrāvī, nārrātum	tell	1

		Conj *Page*
nāscor, nāscī, **nātus sum**	be born	3
nāvigō, nāvigare, nāvigāvī, nāvigātum	sail	1
necō, necāre, necāvī, necātum	kill	1
negō, negāre, negāvī, negātum	refuse/deny	1
neglegō, neglegere, **neglēxi**, **neglēctum**	neglect	3
nesciō, nescīre, nescīvī *or* iī, nescītum	not to know	4
noceō, nocēre, nocuī, nocitum	harm	2
nōlō, **nōlle**, **nōluī**	not to wish/be unwilling	214
nōsco, nōscere, **nōvī**, **nōtum** (in perfect tenses translate as "know")	get to know	3 219
nūntio, nūntiāre, nūntiāvī, nūntiātum	announce	1
obeō, **obīre**, **obīvī** *or* **iī**, **obitum**	die	
obiciō, obicere, **obiēcī**, **obiectum**	throw to/oppose	3
oblīvīscor, oblīvīscī, **oblītus sum**	forget	3
obsideō, obsidēre, **obsēdī**, **obsessum**	besiege	2
obtineō, obtinēre, obtinuī, **obtentum**	hold/obtain	2
occidō, occidere, **occidī**, **occāsum**	fall	3
occīdō, occīdere, **occīdī**, **occīsum**	kill	3
occupō, occupāre, occupāvī, occupātum	seize	1
occurrō, occurrere, **occurrī**, **occursum**	meet	3
ōdī, **ōdisse**	hate	219
offerō, **offerre**, **obtulī**, **oblātum**	present	

		Conj *Page*
oportet, oportēre, oportuit	be proper/ ought	2
opprimō, opprimere, **oppressī,** **oppressum**	crush	**3**
oppugnō, oppugnāre, oppugnāvī, oppugnātum	attack	1
optō, optāre, optāvī, optātum	wish	1
orior, orīrī, **ortus sum**	arise	**4**
orō, orāre, orāvī, orātum	beg/plead	1
ornō, ornāre, ornāvī, ornātum	decorate/equip	1
ostendō, ostendere, **ostendī,** **ostentum**	show	**3**
pācō, pācāre, pācāvī, pācātum	pacify	1
paenitet, paenitēre, paenituit	repent of	2
pandō, pandere, **pandī, passum**	spread out	**3**
parcō, parcere, **pepercī, parsum**	spare	**3**
pareō, parēre, paruī	obey	2
pariō, parere, **peperī, partum**	give birth to	**3**
parō, parāre, parāvī, parātum	prepare	1
pāscō, pāscere, **pāvī, pāstūm**	feed	**3**
patefaciō, patefacere, **patefēcī,** **patefactum**	open	**3**
pateō, patēre, patuī	be open	2
patior, patī, **passus sum**	suffer/allow	**3**
paveō, pavēre, **pavī**	fear	2
pellō, pellere, **pepulī, pulsum**	drive	3
pendeō, pendēre, **pependī** (*intrans*)	hang	**2**
pendō, pendere, **pependī, pēnsum**	weigh/pay	**3**
perdō, perdere, **perdidī, perditum**	lose/destroy	**3**
pereō, perīre, periī, peritum	perish	
perficiō, perficere, **perfēcī,** **perfectum**	complete	**3**

		Conj *Page*
pergō, pergere, **perrēxī**, **perrēctum**	proceed	**3**
permittō, permittere, **permīsī**, **permissum**	allow	3
persuadeō, persuadēre, **persuasī**, **persuasum**	persuade	**2**
pertineō, pertīnēre, pertinuī, **pertentum**	concern	**2**
perturbō, pertūrbāre, perturbāvī, perturbātum	confuse	1
perveniō, pervenīre, **pervēnī**, **perventum**	arrive at	**4**
petō, petere, **petīvī**, **petītum**	seek/ask	**3**
placeō, placēre, placuī, placītum	please	2
placet, placēre, placuit	it seems good	2
polliceor, pollicērī, **pollicitus sum**	promise	2
pōnō, pōnere, **posuī**, **positum**	place/put	**3**
portō, portāre, portāvī, portātum	carry	1
poscō, poscere, **poposcī**	ask for/ demand	3
possum, **posse**, **potui**	to be able	*200*
postulō, postulāre, postulāvī, postulātum	demand	1
potior, potīrī, potitus sum	gain possession of	**4**
praebeō, praebēre, praebuī, praebitum	show	2
praeficiō, praeficere, **praefēci**, **praefēctum**	put in command of	**3**
praestō, praestāre, **praestitī**, **praestatum**	stand out	**1**
premō, premere, **pressī**, **pressum**	press	**3**
prōcēdō, prōcēdere, **prōcessī**, **prōcessum**	advance	**3**

		Conj *Page*
prōdō, prōdere, **prōdidī, prōditum**	betray	3
proficīscor, proficīscī, **profectus sum**	set out	3
prōgredior, prōgredī, **progressus sum**	advance	3
prohibeō, prohibēre, prohibuī, prohibitum	prevent	2
prōmitto, prōmittere, **prōmīsī, prōmissum**	promise	3
prōvideō, prōvidere, **prōvīdī, prōvisum**	take precautions	2
pugnō, pugnāre, pugnāvī, pugnātum	fight	1
pūniō, pūnīre, pūnīvī *or* iī, pūnītum	punish	4
putō, putāre, putāvī, putātum	think	1
quaerō, quaerere, **quaesīvī, quaesītum**	ask/seek	3
queror, querī, **questus sum**	complain	3
quiescō, quiescere, **quiēvī, quiētum**	keep quiet	3
rapiō, rapere, **rapuī, raptum**	snatch/seize	3
recipiō, recipere, **recēpī, receptum**	receive/recover	3
recūsō, recūsāre, recūsāvī, recūsātum	refuse	1
reddō, reddere, **reddidī, redditum**	give back/ return	3
redeō, redīre, redīī, reditum	come back/ return	
redūcō, redūcere, **redūxī, reductum**	bring back	3
regō, regere, **rēxī, rēctum**	rule	3
regredior, regredī, **regressus sum**	retreat	3
relinquō, relinquere, **relīquī, relictum**	leave	3

		Conj *Page*
remittō, remittere, **remīsī**, **remissum**	send back	3
reor, rērī, **ratus sum**	think	2
repellō, repellere, **reppulī**, **repulsum**	drive back	3
reperiō, reperīre, **repperī**, **repertum**	find	4
resistō, resistere, **restitī**	resist	3
respiciō, respicere, **respexī**, **respectum**	look back	3
respondeō, respondēre, **respondī**, **respōnsum**	answer	2
restō, restāre, **restitī**	remain	1
restituō, restituere, **restituī**, **restitūtum**	restore	3
retineō, retinēre, retinuī, **retentum**	hold back	2
rideō, ridēre, **rīsī**, **rīsum**	laugh	2
rogō, rogāre, rogāvī, rogātum	ask	1
rumpō, rumpere, **rūpī**, **ruptum**	burst	3
ruō, ruere, **ruī**, **rutum** (**ruitūrus** – *fut part*)	rush/fall	3
sciō, scīre, **scīvī/iī**, **scītum**	know	4
scrībō, scrībere, **scrīpsī**, **scriptum**	write	3
sēcernō, sēcernere, **secrevī**, **sēcrētum**	set apart	3
secō, secāre, **secuī**, **sectum**	cut	1
sedeō, sedēre, **sēdī**, **sessum**	sit	2
sentiō, sentīre, **sēnsi**, **sēnsum**	feel/perceive	4
sepeliō, sepelīre, sepelīvī, **sepultum**	bury	4
sequor, sequī, **secutūs sum**	follow	3
serō, serere, **sēvī**, **satum**	sow	3
serviō, servīre, servīvī, servītum	serve/be a slave	4
servō, servāre, servāvī, servātum	save	1

		Conj *Page*
simulō, simulāre, simulāvī, simulātum	pretend	1
sinō, sinere, **sīvī**, **situm**	allow	**3**
sistō, sistere, **stitī**, **statum**	set up	**3**
soleō, solēre, **solitus sum**	be used to	**2**
sollicitō, sollicitāre, sollicitāvī, sollicitātum	worry	1
solvō, solvere, **solvī**, **solūtum**	loosen	**3**
sonō, sonāre, **sonuī**, **sonitum**	sound	**1**
spargō, spargere, **sparsī**, **sparsum**	scatter/sprinkle	**3**
spectō, spectāre, spectāvī, spectātum	look at	1
spērō, spērāre, spērāvī, spērātum	hope	1
spoliō, spoliāre, spoliāvī, spoliātum	rob/plunder	1
statuō, statuere, **statuī**, **statūtum**	set up	**3**
sternō, sternere, **strāvī**, **strātum**	cover/ overthrow	**3**
stō, stāre, **stetī**, **stātum**	stand	**1**
struō, struere, **strūxī**, **strūctum**	build	**3**
studeō, studēre, studuī	study	2
suādeō, suādēre, **suāsī**, **suāsum**	advise	**2**
subeō, subīre, subiī, subitum	undergo	
succēdō, succēdere, **successī**, **successum**	go up/relieve	**3**
succurrō, succurrere, succurrī, succursum	help	**3**
sum, esse, fuī, futūrus		196
sūmō, sūmere, **sūmpsī**, **sūmptum**	take	**3**
superō, superāre, superāvī, superātum	overcome	1
supersum, superesse, superfuī	survive	
surgō, surgēre, **surrēxī**, **surrēctum**	rise/get up	**3**
suscipiō, suscipere, **suscēpī**, **susceptum**	undertake	**3**

		Conj *Page*
suspicor, suspicārī, suspicātus sum	suspect	1
sustineō, sustinēre, sustinuī, **sustentum**	sustain	2
taceō, tacēre, tacuī, tacitum	be silent	2
taedet, taedēre, taeduit, **taesum est**	be tired of	2
tangō, tangere, **tetigī**, **tactum**	touch	3
tegō, tegere, **tēxī**, **tectum**	cover	3
tendō, tendere, **tetendī**, **tentum** *or* **tēnsum**	stretch	3
teneō, tenēre, tenuī, **tentum**	hold	2
terreō, terrēre, terruī, territum	terrify	2
timeō, timēre, timuī	fear	2
tollō, tollere, **sustulī**, **sublātum**	raise/remove	3
tonō, tonāre, **tonuī**	thunder	1
torqueō, torquēre, **torsī**, **tortum**	twist	2
trādō, trādere, **trādidī**, **trāditum**	hand over	3
trahō, trahere, **trāxī**, **tractum**	drag	3
traicio, traicere, **traieci**, **traiectum**	take across	3
trānseō, trānsīre, trānsiī, trānsitum	cross over	
tueor, tuērī, tuitus sum	look at	2
ulcīscor, ulcīscī, **ultus sum**	punish/avenge	3
urgeō, urgēre, **ursī**	press/urge	2
urō, urere, **ussī**, **ustum**	burn	3
ūtor, ūtī, **ūsus sum**	use	3
valeō, valēre, valuī, valitum	be strong	2
vastō, vastāre, vastāvī, vastātum	destroy	1
vehō, vehere, **vēxī**, **vectum**	carry	3
vendō, vendere, **vendidī**, **venditum**	sell	3
veniō, venīre, **vēnī**, **ventum**	come	4
vereor, verērī, veritus sum	fear	2

		Conj *Page*
vertō, vertere, **vertī**, **versum**	turn	**3**
vescor, vescī	feed on	3
vetō, vetāre, **vetuī**, **vetitum**	forbid	**1**
videō, vidēre, **vīdī**, **vīsum**	see	**2**
vigilō, vigilāre, vigilāvī, vigilātum	stay awake	1
vinciō, vincīre, **vinxī**, **vinctum**	bind	**4**
vincō, vincere, **vīcī**, **victum**	defeat/conquer	**3**
vitō, vitāre, vitāvī, vitātum	avoid	1
vivō, vivere, **vīxī**, **victum**	live	**3**
vocō, vocāre, vocāvī, vocātum	call/invite	1
volō, velle, voluī	wish/want	*212*
volvō, volvere, **volvī**, **volūtum**	roll	**3**
voveō, vovēre, **vōvī**, **vōtum**	vow	**2**

The following index lists comprehensively both grammatical terms and key words in English and Latin.